# Challenges

## Global learning in a globalised world

edited by Engelbert Thaler

Iris Edelbrock
Birgit Schmidt-Grob

# Advertising and Marketing – Products, Promises and Persuasion

Schöningh

**Task 3:**
Watch the film *What women want* and find out about the development and composition of a commercial.

Strategy Sheet 12, p. 23
Info Sheet 13, p. 24
Text 14, p. 25
Worksheet 15, p. 26
Worksheet 16, p. 28

**Task 4:**
Exchange your personal experiences as consumers and become aware of legal and illegal sales practices.

Text 17, p. 29

**Task 5:**
Activate and practice your communication skills, and perform a role play as "salesmen".

Worksheet 18, p. 30

# Aspect 4:

## "It's all illusion ..." – Marketing and sales in literature (pp. 32–39)

**Task 1:**
Read the excerpt from Tennessee Williams' play *The last of my solid gold watches*, and find out how salesmanship and sales practices have changed over time.

Text 19, p. 33
Worksheet 20, p. 35

**Task 2:**
Reflect on the purpose and effect of rhymes, as referred to in the extract from Aldous Huxley's utopian novel *Brave new world*.

Worksheet 21, p. 37

**Task 3:**
Become aware of how the film industry makes use of product placement as a means of promotion, and read the excerpt from the screenplay *The Truman show*.

Worksheet 22, p. 38

# Aspect 5:

## No limits at all? – How advertising influences people (pp. 40–49)

**Task 1:**
Experience how advertising strategies change in order to meet new trends and changing attitudes.

Text 23, p. 41
Text 24, p. 42

**Task 2:**
Consumer protection versus freedom of advertising: discuss the pros and cons in a debate.

Worksheet 25, p. 43

**Task 3:**
Analyse how Hollywood celebrities are used to promote cars, and design your own commercial starring famous actors and VIPs.

Worksheet 26, p. 45

**Task 4:**
Learn about marketing campaigns that went wrong and came to nothing.

Text 27, p. 46
Text 28, p. 47

**Task 5:**
Become aware of how politics create public images and adjust truth/reality to necessities. Do political campaigning yourself and create catchy slogans.

Text 29, p. 48
Strategy Sheet 30, p. 49

# Zur Konzeption

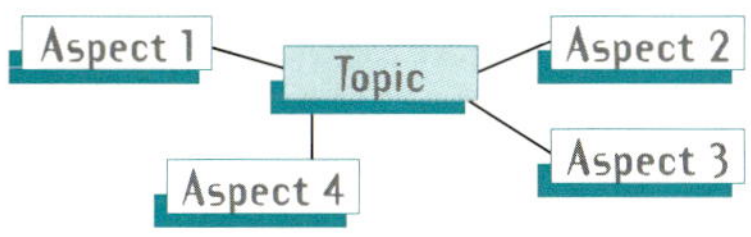


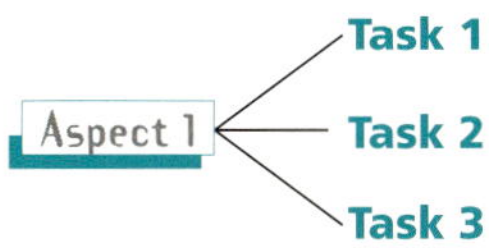


Die Reihe **Challenges – Global learning in a globalised world** stellt zu den 3 Gs des Phänomens Globalisierung (Grundwerte, Gefahren, Gelegenheiten) aktuelle Materialien in Form von Unterrichtsmodellen für den Englischunterricht zusammen. Die Perspektive der praktizierenden Lehrkraft steht dabei im Vordergrund. Deshalb wurde besonderer Wert auf eine übersichtliche Struktur der Hefte gelegt.

- Jedes Thema (**Topic**) gliedert sich in mehrere **Aspects**. Ein Aspect ist in sich abgeschlossen, sodass er auch separat behandelt werden kann.
- Der Lernprozess wird – in Anlehnung an das Konzept des Task-Based Language Learning – durch Aufgaben (**Tasks**) strukturiert. Ein Task ist eine resultatsorientierte Aufgabenstellung mit kommunikativem oder linguistischem Fokus.
  Aspects und Tasks werden in einer Übersicht zu Beginn auf den **ausklappbaren Seiten 4 und 5** des Heftes dargestellt. Hier kann man sich schnell einen Überblick über den Ablauf des Unterrichts verschaffen.
- Der Einstieg in das Gesamtthema des Heftes erfolgt über eine **Getting started-Aktivität** (Seiten 6 und 7).
- Jeder Aspect beginnt mit **Hinweisen für den Unterricht:** Tipps zur Umsetzung, Alternativen, Bezugsquellen, Tafelbilder.
- Es folgen die **Kopiervorlagen** des Aspects:
  - Arbeitsblätter (Worksheets)
  - Sach-Informationen (Info Sheets)
  - Infos zu Unterrichtsmethoden (Method Sheets)
  - Lern- und Arbeitsstrategien für die Schüler (Strategy Sheets)
  - Texte, Bilder, Grafiken usw. (Texts)
- Jedes Heft wird mit einer **Review**, die Gelerntes nochmals zusammenfasst, abgeschlossen.
- **Klausurvorschläge** am Ende des Heftes erleichtern die Unterrichtsvorbereitung.

**Herausgeber:**
Prof. Dr. Engelbert Thaler
**Autorinnen des Heftes:**
Iris Edelbrock, Birgit Schmidt-Grob
**Sprachliche Betreuung:**
Alexandra Rieb



www.schoeningh-schulbuch.de
Schöningh Verlag, Jühenplatz 1–3, 33098 Paderborn



Druck 5 4 3 2 1 / Jahr 2012 11 10 09 08
Die letzte Zahl bezeichnet das Jahr dieses Druckes.

Umschlaggestaltung: Ivonne Junge-Illies, Mannheim
Druck und Bindung: AZ Druck und Datentechnik GmbH/Kempten (Allgäu)

ISBN 978-3-14-040210-1

# Aspects of Advertising and Marketing

## Aspect 1:

### The basics of advertising – A workshop approach (pp. 8–15)

**Task 1:**
In the economy of Western Europe consumer goods are easily available – there is a surplus of mostly everything. Reflect on which products you buy for your daily needs and which items you buy because of advertising or just for fun.

**Task 2:**
Learn about advertising and marketing strategies and their instruments and do the various activities on the worksheet.

Worksheet 1, p. 9
Worksheet 2, p. 10

**Task 3:**
Use advertising strategies and design your own ad.

Strategy Sheet 3, p. 12
Strategy Sheet 4, p. 13
Worksheet 5, p. 14
Strategy Sheet 6, p. 15

## Aspect 2:

### Marketing – Launching a product on the market (pp. 16–21)

**Task 1:**
Prepare your own advertising campaign and learn about the "new product development funnel".

Info Sheet 7, p. 17

**Task 2:**
Learn about promotion techniques to make a product/message more convincing.

Info Sheet 8, p. 18

**Task 3:**
Do a project in groups: Develop your own product, launch it on the market, and run your own advertising campaign.

Info Sheet 9, p. 19
Strategy Sheet 10, p. 20
Worksheet 11, p. 21

## Aspect 3:

### Action! – Advertising and sales in the movies (pp. 22–31)

**Task 1:**
Improve your rhetorical skills and your advertising and marketing vocabulary.

Strategy Sheet 12, p. 23
Strategy Sheet 3, p. 12

**Task 2:**
Discuss in class: which commercials and ads promoting sports equipment (e.g. sneakers, dresses, etc.) do you recall, and what is their specific message and target group?

# Contents

# Getting started

Remove advertising, disable a person or firm from proclaiming its wares and their merits, and the whole of society and of the economy is transformed. The enemies of advertising are the enemies of freedom.
*David Ogilvy, US businessman (1911–1999)*

With public opinion on its side, nothing can fail.
*Abraham Lincoln, US President (1809–1865)*

Advertising is the very essence of democracy. An election goes on every minute of the business day across the counters of hundreds of thousands of stores and shops where the customers state their preferences and determine which manufacturer and which product shall be the leader today, and which shall lead tomorrow.
*Bruce Barton, US advertising executive (1886–1967)*

**1.** Compare the DKNY ad and the painting *Adam and Eve* by Lucas Cranach the Elder (1526). What do both pictures have in common? What is their message?

**2.** Discuss the given statements in class as well as the pros and cons of advertisements.

**3.** Have you ever bought a product because it was promoted by a particular advert or commercial? If yes, which products?

**4.** What is the product behind the slogan? Make a guess.

**5.** Which of the slogans do you like/dislike – and why?

**6.** What stylistic "tricks" are employed in the slogans to make them interesting and conspicuous for the customer?

(1) Be the first to know.
(2) Whenever you need to know.
(3) Keeping you ahead of the storm.
(4) Make the most of now.
(5) Connecting people.
(6) Buy it. Sell it. Love it.
(7) Solutions for a small planet.
(8) Your potential, our passion.
(9) Always low prices.
(10) Higher standards, lower prices.
(11) Impossible is nothing.
(12) Just do it.
(13) Life is short. Play hard.
(14) Guarantees for the if in life.
(15) Live richly.
(16) The heart of commerce.
(17) You don't have to be rich, just smart.
(18) Because I'm worth it.
(19) Your fragrance. Your rules.
(20) Plop, plop, fizz, fizz, oh what a relief it is!
(21) Tough on grease. Soft on hands.
(22) We love having you here.
(23) Make the dream come true.
(24) The Happiest Place on Earth.
(25) Spend a night, not a fortune.
(26) Just plane smart.
(27) We really move our tail for you.
(28) The Heartbeat of America.
(29) Think small.
(30) ZoomZoom
(31) Men at their best.
(32) Forever new frontiers.

**(1)** CNN International **(2)** BBC News **(3)** The Weather Channel **(4)** Vodafone **(5)** Nokia **(6)** eBay **(7)** IBM **(8)** Microsoft **(9)** Wal-Mart **(10)** Meijer food and retail store chain **(11)** Adidas **(12)** Nike **(13)** Reebok **(14)** MetLife insurance **(15)** Citibank **(16)** MasterCard **(17)** IKEA (USA) **(18)** L'Oréal **(19)** Hugo Boss **(20)** Alka-Seltzer **(21)** Palmolive **(22)** Hampton Inn (Hotel chain) **(23)** Walt Disney World **(24)** Disneyland **(25)** Econo Lodge (cheap motel chain) **(26)** Southwest Airlines **(27)** Continental Airlines **(28)** Chevrolet **(29)** Volkswagen Beetle (1962) **(30)** Mazda **(31)** Pakistan Army **(32)** Boeing

# Aspect 1: The basics of advertising – A workshop approach

**Task 1: In the economy of Western Europe consumer goods are easily available – there is a surplus of mostly everything. Reflect on which products you buy for your daily needs and which items you buy because of advertising or just for fun.**

Indem die Schülerinnen und Schüler reflektieren und wahrnehmen, wie groß die Diskrepanz ist zwischen dem tatsächlichen Bedarf an Konsumgütern des alltäglichen Gebrauchs und den zusätzlichen „Luxusgütern", deren Notwendigkeit dem Konsumenten über Werbung vermittelt wird, werden sie für die Thematik sensibilisiert. In Form eines Schreibgespräches kann über die Frage „(Why) do we need advertising?" nachgedacht werden. Dazu wird die o. g. Frage auf einen Flip-Chart-Bogen geschrieben. Weitere Flip-Chart-Bögen können z. B. die (provokativen) Statements "Advertising is a waste of time and money" oder "Advertising is a mayor instrument of the economy" erhalten. Die Plakate werden so auf Tischen ausgelegt, dass die Schülerinnen und Schüler darum herumgehen und ihre Kommentare stumm darauf schreiben können; dafür haben sie ca. 20–30 Minuten Zeit. Auch die Kommentare von Mitschülern können schriftlich kommentiert und ergänzt werden. Daran anschließen sollte sich eine Besprechung der Statements und gegebenenfalls eine Gewichtung und weitere Erörterung der jeweiligen Aspekte.

**Task 2: Learn about advertising and marketing strategies and their instruments and do the various activities on the worksheet.**

Mithilfe der Worksheets 1 und 2 (S. 9f.) erhalten die Schülerinnen und Schüler erste Grundinformationen über die wesentlichen Elemente von Werbeanzeigen, die sie zur Überprüfung und Bewertung von Werbung in Printmedien einsetzen können. Worksheet 1 kann auch zum Einstieg als OHP-Folie eingesetzt werden und/oder stummer Impuls für ein Unterrichtsgespräch. Empfehlenswerte weitere Literatur zum Thema ist: Erica Levin, *Write Great Ads – A Step-by-Step Approach,* Wiley & Sons, New York, 1990; James B. Twitchell, *Adcult USA – The Triumph of Advertising in American Culture,* Columbia University Press, New York, 1996 sowie der Klassiker: David Ogilvy, *Ogilvy on Advertising,* Vintage Books, New York, 1983. Auch die Website http://english.unitecnology.ac.nz/resources/resources/advertising.html bietet vielseitige Informationen und Vokabellisten zum Themenbereich *Advertising*.

**Task 3: Use advertising strategies and design your own ad.**

Um den Blick der Schülerinnen und Schüler aus der Konsumentenperspektive heraus auf die praktische Umsetzbarkeit und den praktischen Nutzen von Werbetechniken im Alltag zu lenken, soll hier ein Stellenangebot zum Anlass genommen werden, eine (Werbe-) Anzeige zu gestalten. Dies kann ebenfalls in (arbeitsteiliger) Gruppenarbeit erfolgen. Unter Zuhilfenahme der Strategy Sheets 3 und 4 (S. 12 f.) sowie des Worksheets 5 (S. 14) entwickeln die Schülerinnen und Schüler *Adverts* für unterschiedliche Zwecke (z. B. *job application, offering a service, etc.).* Diese Übung kann auch als Vorbereitung für das Projekt *Advertising Campaign* in Aspect 2 (S. 20 ff.) genutzt werden. Zusätzlich werden Bewerbungsbriefe (Strategy Sheet 6, S.15) verfasst. Idealerweise lässt man die Schülerinnen und Schüler zunächst ein formal korrektes Schreiben verfassen und im Anschluss daran (z. B. als Hausaufgabe) ein humorvolles und kreatives Anschreiben, das den (ironischen) Ton des Stellenangebotes aufgreift. Für die erste Arbeitsphase sollten *Dictionaries* bereitgestellt werden, die sowohl bei Vokabularfragen als auch bei der formalen Gestaltung helfen. Einen schönen Abschluss könnte ein Klassenprojekt bilden, in dem die erstellten Stellenangebote/-gesuche in Form einer Wandzeitung zusammengefügt und ausgestellt werden.

**1.** Describe the advert: What is the "product" sold in this advert? What is the ad's message?

**2.** What are the basic elements of this advert?

**3.** Which information does the body copy provide about consumer habits – and how advertising should meet these needs? Do you think this information is true?

**4.** Devise your own definition of the terms "advertising" and "marketing".

# The basic elements of an advertisement

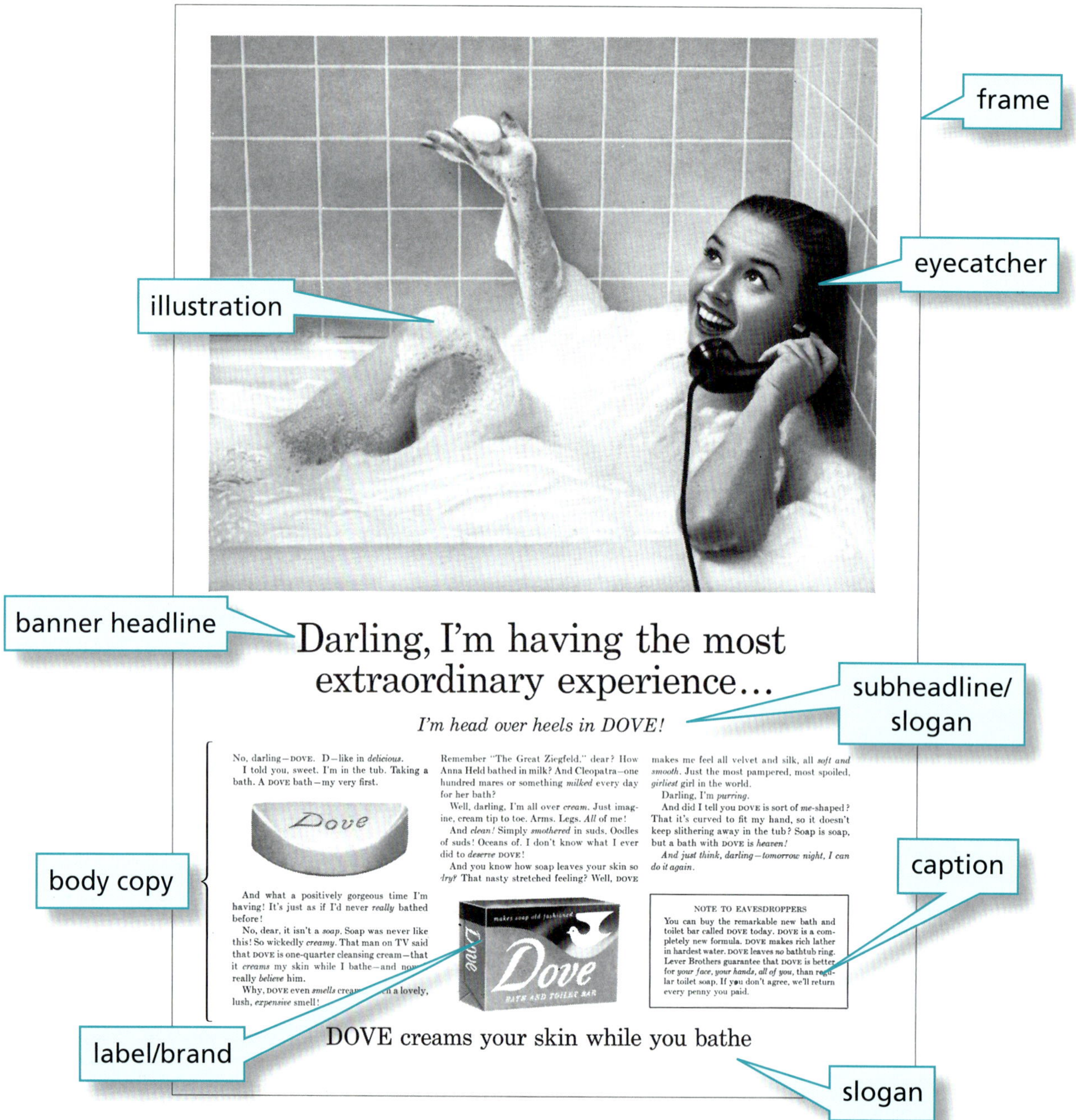


Collect adverts from different newspapers and magazines and bring them to school.

**1.** Examine their elements and messages.

How do they aim at:

- attracting people's attention,
- evoking emotions and desires,
- influencing people and making them want to buy the product?

**2.** How informative are the ads – which detailed information is given about the product's quality?

**3.** Discuss the quality and impact of various ads in groups and develop criteria for evaluating ads.

**1.** • big picture: Moses bringing two stone tablets with the engraving of the 10 commandments from Mount Sinai; below: a slogan and a text; in the bottom-right corner is a caption reading "Advertising"; picture looks like an old-fashioned print/wood engraving

- the motif is chosen from the Bible/Old Testament: the advert mocks the impact of adverts – even the strongest/most powerful message might be left unheard because of the wrong advertising strategy; there is a pun/play on words on the word "buy": a) to obtain sth by paying money for it and b) (*infml*) to believe that sth is true

**2.** a large picture; a slogan in capital letters in bold print; a text (body copy) arranged in three columns below the slogan; the caption "Advertising"; two bottom lines: the publisher/source

**3.**

| Consumer habits | Advertising strategy |
|---|---|
| • overwhelming tendency to question things they are told<br>• people make their own decisions<br>• people are very individual<br>• they claim to be influenced by ads<br>• ads make them buy things they don't want | • simply presenting facts<br>• trying to make facts interesting and entertaining<br>• then waiting and hoping they got through to the customer<br>• has only a limited impact on people's actions<br>• advertising = freedom of choice |

**4.** **Advertising:** A marketing process which uses advertisements directed to prospects as a means of meeting marketing objectives; as a marketing tool, advertising is uniquely able to reliably and quickly deliver consistent messages efficiently. Advertising is typically done with signs, brochures, commercials, direct mailings, e-mail messages or personal contact.

**Marketing:** Marketing is a wide range of activities involved in making sure that you are continuing to meet the needs of your customers and getting value in return. Marketing is usually focused on one product or service. Marketing activities include "inbound marketing", such as market research to find out, for example, what groups of potential customers exist, what their needs are, which of these needs you can meet, how you should meet them, etc. Inbound marketing also includes analysing the competition, positioning your new product or service (finding your market niche), and pricing your products and services. "Outbound marketing" includes promoting a product through continued advertising, promotions, public relations and sales.

---

Erwartungshorizont
Worksheet
2

**1.** various results; the students should present their findings on posters and give reasons for their judgements

**2.** students should list the information given and check how reliable/trustworthy/true or detailed it actually is (e. g. price, quality, use/function, etc.)

**3.** • Who is the target customer? Does the advert appeal to him/her?

- Does the advert meet the needs of the market / the customer's needs and desires?
- Does the advert evoke new desires and create the incentive to buy the particular product/service?

Possible criteria:

| design | liability of information | quality of the given information | language | chosen motifs |
|---|---|---|---|---|
| | | | | |

# How to create a catchy slogan

**In order to create a catchy slogan or ad, experimenting and playing with words and sounds and their (different) meanings is very helpful.**

- Work in teams, and try to imagine and visualize the product you want to write about. Which characteristics, sounds, colours, smells, surroundings, etc. come to your mind?
- Look up words in a dictionary and write everything down on a big piece of paper.
- Exchange ideas and connect words/expressions that you like best.

| | |
|---|---|
| **Onomatopoeia** (= words containing sounds similar to the words they describe) | hiss, plop, pop, bang, squeeze, ooze, oozy (liquid), fizz, fuzz, splash, buzz(er), sizzle, dribble, etc. |
| **Rhyming/rhythm** | well-sell, shop-drop, nice-price, eye-rhyme, etc. |
| **Alliterations** (= the use of the same letter/sound at the beginning of words that are close together) | sensational summer sales ..., best bargain buy ..., etc. |
| **Neologisms** (= new word/expression or a new meaning of a word, new combinations of words) | best-buy, silk-soft, must-have, frappucchino, feelgood, etc. |
| **Puns** (= the clever or humorous use of a word that has more than one meaning, or of words that have different meanings but sound the same: wordplay) | plane-plain, game-gain: tail-tale, dressing-dressing, jeans-genes, etc. |
| **Proverbs** (= a well-known phrase or sentence that gives advice or says sth that is generally true) | A stitch in time saves nine./A man's home is his castle./First come, first served./Happy wife, happy life./etc. |
| **Speeding up** (= using short, monosyllabic words) | in, out, super, great, best, just, buy, now, cheap, safe, clean, fast, come, go, etc. |
| **Slowing down** (= using long, polysyllabic words) | extraordinary, magnificent, inexpensive, sensational, exclusively, glamorous, purchase, immediately, etc. |
| **Superlatives** | best, most, only, unique, easiest, simplest, greatest, exclusively, etc. |
| **Comparatives** | better than, more than, larger ..., cheaper ..., etc. |
| **(Suggestive) questions/(rhetorical) questions** | Do you suffer from ... ?, What if ... ?, Why are ... ?, Why not ... ?, etc. |
| **Foreign words/technical terms ("expert language")** | frappé, latte, fragrance, chronograph/chronometer, vintage, accessories, etc. |
| **Prefixes** | extra- ..., mega- ..., etc. |

# Write and design your own ad

**The five fundamentals:**

1. **Get attention**
   Headline, picture, provocation, attraction, superlative, question, colours, news …

2. **Show people an advantage**
   Better health, more money, more comfort, greater popularity, more safety, more leisure, pride of accomplishment, social advancement, business advancement …

3. **Prove it**
   Facts, reputation, long-experienced personnel statements, experts, quality, patents, delivery, speed, duration, commendations, testimony of users, credibility …

4. **Persuade people to grasp this advantage**
   Desirability, a special bargain, emphasizing the advantages …

5. **Ask for action**
   Making a special offer, time limit, price going up, gain or loss, guarantee …
   Give information which makes it easier for people to act immediately: give the exact location/address, a drawing of a map, opening hours, full details of easy payment-plans, mail-order coupons …

**Power words for headlines and retail products:**

| Headlines | Retail products | 4 functions of a headline |
|---|---|---|
| now, today, immediately, free, money, save, love, health, safe, proven, results, bonus, learn, know, understand, you, protect, create, trust, powerful, help, profit, dynamic, discover … | new, sensational, energy, clean, convenient, organic, healthy, environment (-friendly), better, faster, cheaper, bigger, economic, delicious, low fat, sporty, dynamic, individual … | • get attention<br>• target the audience<br>• deliver a complete message<br>• draw the reader into the body copy |

**Make use of the "Z" form:**

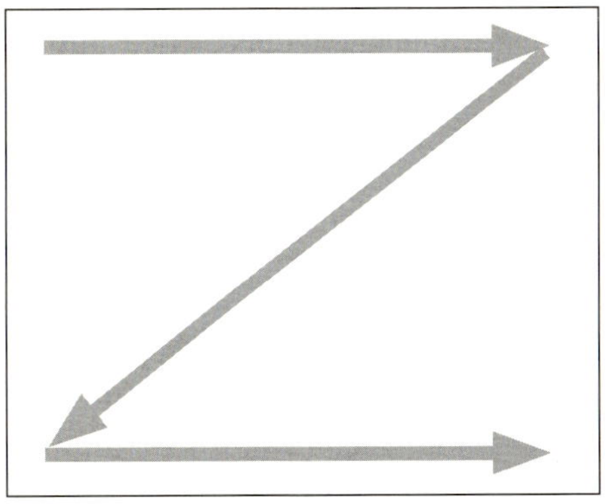

According to one theory, your eyes will scan over the page from left-to-right in a "Z" form unless a design element directs your attention elsewhere. Marketing firms use this theory to place ad elements where they will catch your eyes. There will be an element to lead your eyes in, something catchy in the middle, and the message or logo will frequently appear in the lower-middle area to the right.

# Application for a job – Advertisement

Hamleys
REGENT STREET
THE FINEST TOYSHOP IN THE WORLD

## Action man needed to protect Teddy from the forces of evil.

### Security Guards
### £8,800 pa plus benefits

Hamleys enjoys a unique reputation as the finest toy store in the world and they're looking for Security Guards who can uphold that reputation.

You will be working in shifts from 7.00am to 7.00pm. Ideally you have experience of working in a retail environment and you have an in-depth knowledge of P.A.C.E.

You are smart in appearance, you have good references and even better eyesight. Hamleys is a very busy store, so rest assured that Teddy, the Cabbage Patch Kids and Masters of the Universe will keep you on your toes.

If you're interested in being a Security Guard with Hamleys, write enclosing relevant details to The Personnel Department, Hamleys, 188-196 Regent Street, London W1R 6BT. Telephone: 01-734 3161.

***This position is open to Wonder Women as well as Action Men.***

## Job Description

Seeking **young women** willing to work long hours, for low pay, without protective gear, seven days a week, sometimes 24 hours in a row. Ability to deal with stress a plus. Union activists need not apply.

| | |
|---|---|
| **Job** | Sewing jeans an other clothes for Pepe, Guess, Wrangler, Tommy, the Gap and Burton. You and your 700 colleagues will sew 500.000 pieces a month for customers in the UK, Ireland, France, Belgium, the Netherlands and the United States. |
| **Equipment** | Sewing machines and stools. |
| **Place of work** | Hong Kong owned factory in Mauritius. View over busy industrial estate from windows that don't open. |
| **Hours** | Seven days a week. |
| **Housing** | Nearby or inside the factory. |
| **Benefits** | A multicultural experience. You'll meet other workers, some who have travelled all the way from China! |

**Contact us now!**

aus: „Unterrichtsmaterialien Englisch betrifft uns" Ausgabe 2/2007 "Globalization" © Bergmoser + Höller Verlag AG, Aachen

**1.** Choose one of the two ads offering jobs/posts in London and Mauritius and write:

a) a formal letter of application and

b) an informal, more creatively designed letter/ad in which you apply for the offered job/post/position.

**2.** Design your own job advertisement/description (e. g. looking for a summer job, looking for participants in your drama club, a flyer, a poster, a newspaper ad, etc.).

**Tip:** Use the study pages of your dictionary (usually at the end of the dictionary), which offer help on how to write a formal letter and a CV (curriculum vitae).

# How to write a formal letter and CV (curriculum vitae)

> your own address in top right hand corner

Tel: 07654 5600

Am oberen Hügel 29
70000 Stuttgart
Germany

15th May 2007

Your ref: TBS/1234

> address in full, as on envelope

Mr Smith
The Personnel Department, Hamleys
188–196 Regent Street
London W1R6BT
Great Britain

> Use "Madam or Sir" if you do not know the name of the person.

Dear Mr Smith,

> introductory paragraph; reason for your letter

I am writing to apply for the post of a Security Guard advertised in The Guardian of May 12.
Please find enclosed a copy of my CV.

> body of letter; your qualifications; reason why you want the job

Since graduating from St. Michael's Grammar School I have been doing work practice, protecting parking lots of various companies. I have become particularly interested in department stores focusing on toys and pets.

I would welcome the chance to work for your company and look forward to hearing from you.

Yours sincerely,

> Sign your name and print it in full afterwards.

K. Sonnenschein

Karin Sonnenschein

**Curriculum Vitae**

| | |
|---|---|
| **Name** | Karin Sonnenschein |
| **Address** | Am oberen Hügel 29<br>70000 Stuttgart |
| **Telephone No.** | 07654 5600 |
| **Mobile** | 01723456789 |
| **Email** | ksunshine@web.de |
| **Nationality** | German |
| **Date/place of birth** | 25th July 1992 in Cologne |
| **Profile** | A highly motivated and creative graduate with experience in protection. |
| **Education** | |
| 1996–1999 | Elementary School |
| 1999–2007 | Grammar School (A-Level) |
| **Employment/ Experience** | Surveillance and protection of parking lots |
| **Interests** | Judo, tennis, music |

**Useful expressions**

- I noted with interest ...
- I am writing in response to ...
- With reference to your advertisement in ...

- As you will see from my CV ...
- I am currently studying ... at ...
- After gaining a degree, I ...
- This post interests me because ...

- I would be grateful for the opportunity to improve my skills ...
- I have extensive experience of ...

- I am available for interview ...
- If you consider that my qualifications are suitable ...

# Aspect 2: Marketing – Launching a product on the market

**Task 1: Prepare your advertising campaign and learn about the "new product development funnel".**

Das Info Sheet 7 (S. 17) gibt einen konzentrierten Überblick über die notwendigen Schritte zur Produktentwicklung und Vermarktung. Es kann, auf OHP-Folie kopiert, als Einstieg in das Projekt (S. 19 ff.) dienen und einen ersten (Gesprächs-) Anreiz bilden, die weiteren Schritte vorzubereiten.

**Task 2: Learn about promotion techniques to make a product/message more convincing.**

Um ein Produkt erfolgreich am Markt zu platzieren, bedarf es nicht nur einer zielgerichteten Werbekampagne, sondern auch weiterer *promotion techniques* (Info Sheet 8, S. 18). Ergänzend zur Thematisierung der Techniken im Unterricht kann von den Schülerinnen und Schülern auch eine „Vor-Ort-Recherche" betrieben werden (z. B. im Kaufhaus, Supermarkt), deren Ergebnisse dann in der Klasse vorgestellt und diskutiert werden.

**Task 3: Do a project in groups: Develop your own product, launch it on the market, and run your own advertising campaign.**

In arbeitsteiliger Gruppenarbeit sollen die Schülerinnen und Schüler schließlich ihre erworbenen Kompetenzen praktisch anwenden und in Form eines Projektes selbst ein Produkt ersinnen und „auf den Markt bringen". Dafür werden 3 Worksheets bereitgestellt, die die notwendigen Informationen für die Produktentwicklung, die Aufgabenstellungen sowie Aspekte der Marktanalyse vermitteln:

Worksheet 9 (S. 19): Developing and launching a product
Strategy Sheet 10 (S. 20): Developing a product and planning an advertising compaign
Worksheet 11 (S. 21): Task cards

Entscheidend ist, dass jedes Team schließlich ein (vorzeigbares) Produkt entwickelt hat – es sollte hier nicht nur theoretisierend, sondern ganz praktisch gearbeitet werden. Dabei dürfen die Schülerinnen und Schüler ihrer Fantasie freien Lauf lassen – solange sie sich an die Bedingungen der Aufgabenstellung halten. Neben der Produktentwicklung ist auch die Präsentation wichtig – welches Medium (TV/Radio Commercial, Ad, Poster, etc.) gewählt wird, steht in freiem Belieben. Abschließend könnte im Plenum die Frage erörtert werden, wodurch ein Produkt am Markt zum Bestseller oder Flop wird und welche Mechanismen dies möglicherweise beeinflussen (siehe Worksheet 1, S. 9).

# New product development funnel

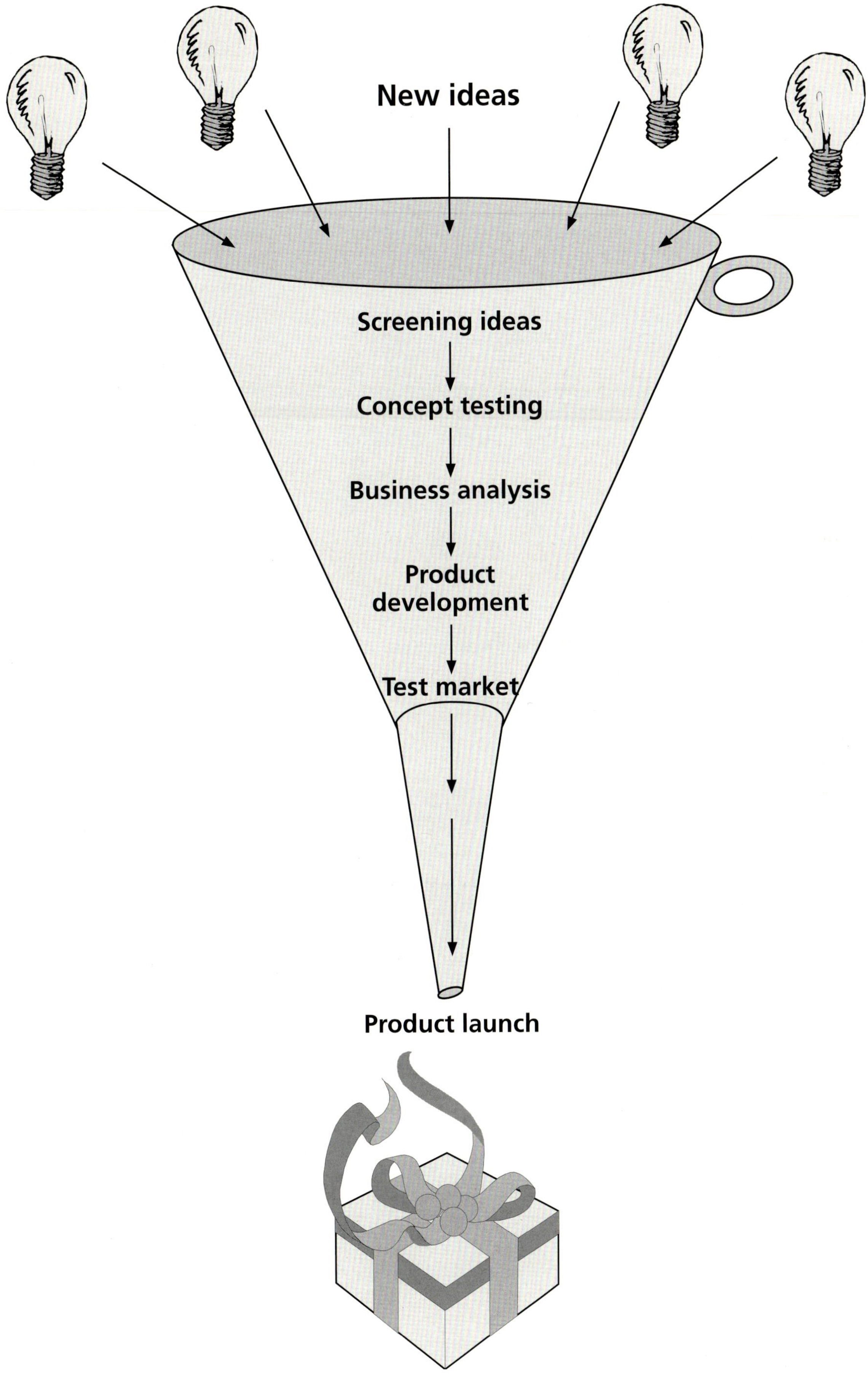

# Promotional techniques and tricks of the trade

To increase sales or to introduce a new product promotional techniques are used, in addition to advertising – usually at the point of sale.

**Trading stamps**
These are given to the customer in proportion to the amount spent. Full books of stamps can be exchanged for goods or cash.

**Coupons or vouchers**
These allow the customer to buy another package of the same product at a reduced price. The coupons are often inside the package or printed on the outside. The customer has to collect them before he can get the cheap offer.

**Extras**
Customers may be given an extra tin or packet 'free' if they buy a certain number at full price. Sometimes a manufacturer will attach a miniature package of the product to induce people to buy.

**Gifts**
These may be very cheap free articles given with the product. Often you can buy an expensive article of another firm at a reduced price when you send a certain number of wrappers, caps or coupons.

**Star offer/Best bargain**
These are goods which sold at a very reduced price to attract the people to the shop. Sometimes you also get 'special offers' when you buy products in bulk.

**Competitions**
They often come with expensive prizes. The entry form is usually inside the package or printed on the outside so that people have to buy the product before they can enter.

adapted from Commerce in Action by Peter & Joan Moss by permission of Paterson Marsh Ltd

# Project: Developing and launching a product

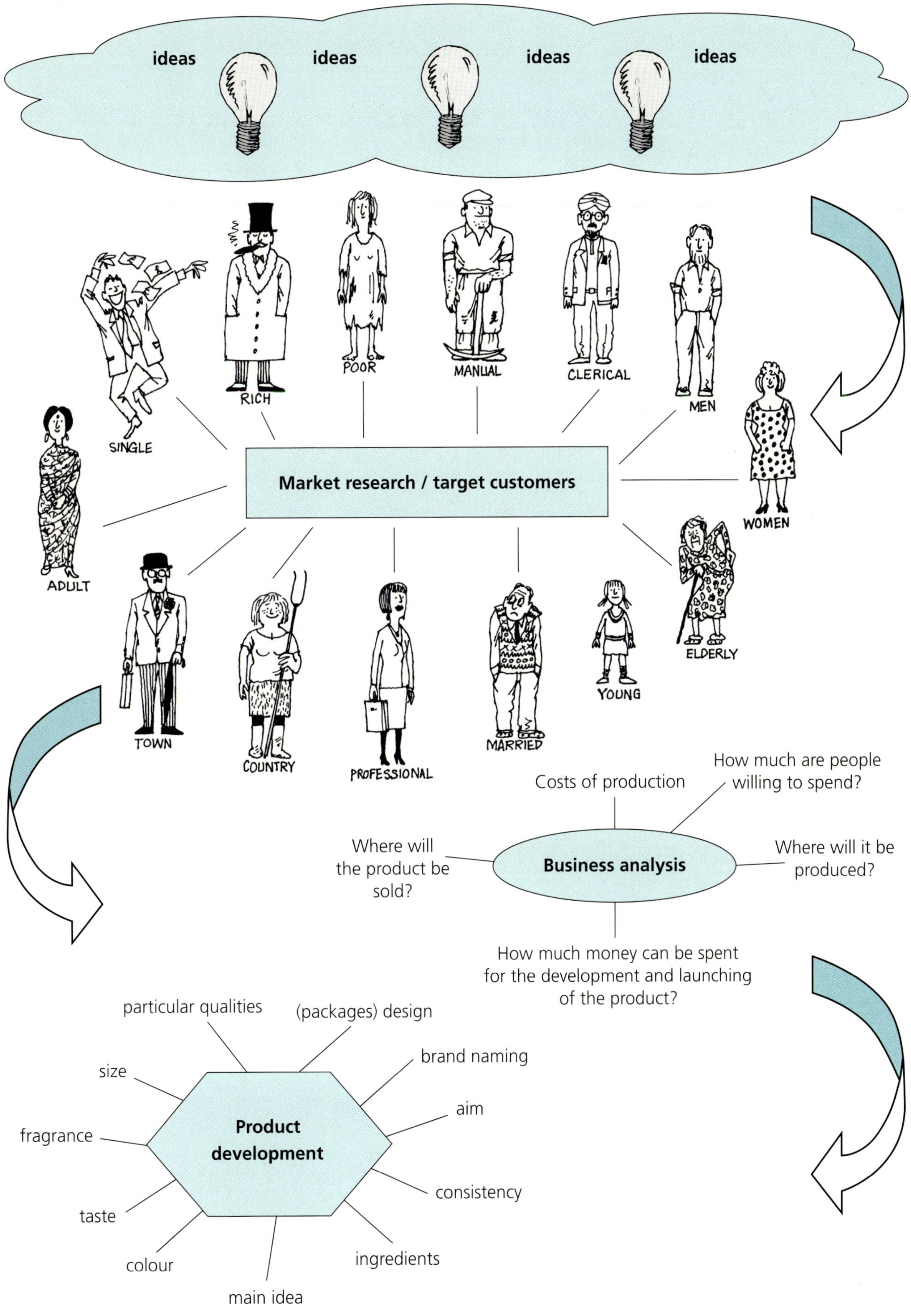

# Developing a product and planning an advertising campaign

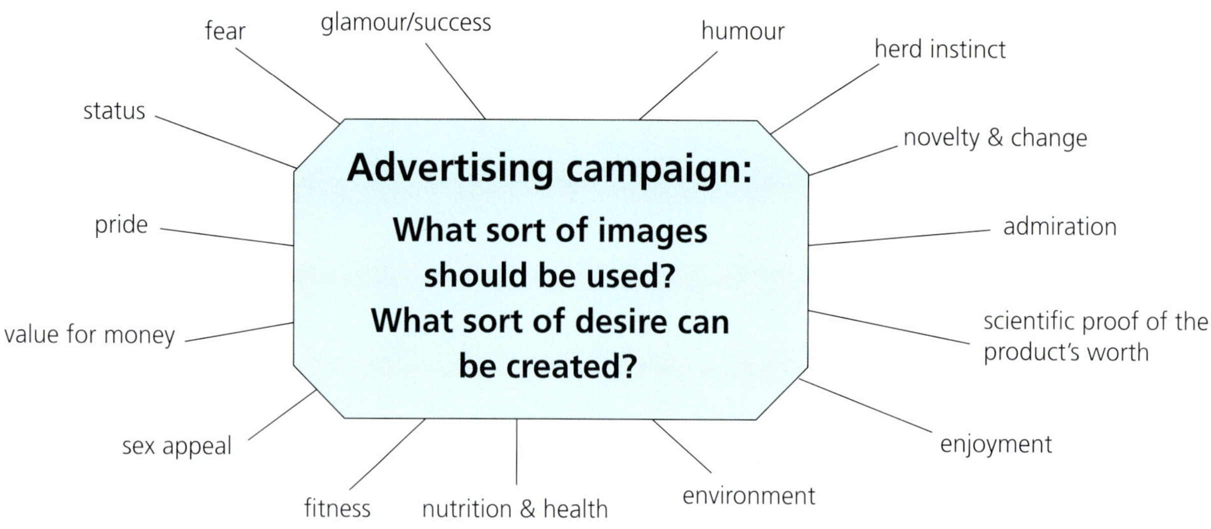


Form 4 to 7 groups that work on creating and launching a product.
Use the information and material provided.
Decide on which product you are going to create and launch, and choose from these (raw) materials:

1. milk
2. olive oil
3. sugar beets
4. cotton
5. perfume
6. hemp

It is your task to **design and run an advertising campaign**.
Your final **presentation** should include the following aspects:

- presentation of the product
- definition of the target consumer
- explanation of the function/quality of the product
- explanation of the product's design (and packaging)
- place(s) of production
- your marketing strategy and media employed

You should be able to explain and justify your decisions by, for example, referring to market needs, surplus of production, unemployment, improvement of a product, environmental problems, etc.

# Tasks for the product development and advertising campaign

## TEAM 1

**Situation:** The production of **premium quality cotton** is facing severe backdrops on the international market. The economic situation of cotton farmers in the USA and in India is alarming.

**Task:** Your team is asked to develop a product that serves the needs and trends of the market and at the same time considers the situation mentioned above.

## TEAM 2

**Situation:** In the south of Spain millions of olive trees have been cut down and the region is expecting an ecological disaster. At the same time the demand for **olive oil** for haute cuisine and premium quality cosmetic products made of olive oil is increasing.

**Task:** Develop a product that supports the consumption of olive oil and thereby enables farmers in Spain to replant trees and support ecology.

## TEAM 3

**Situation:** In many regions in Germany farmers suffer from an overproduction of **sugar beets** and a drop-off of prices at which they can sell their products.

**Task:** Your team is to develop a new product that involves the use of sugar beets.

## TEAM 4

**Situation:** Since the release of the film "The Perfume" consumer demand for fragrances has been rising dramatically.

**Task:** Your team is asked to develop a new product, **cosmetic or fragrance**, that meets the demands of the market.

## TEAM 5

**Situation:** Politics have legalized the production of **hemp**, as it is a multifunctional and environment-friendly plant that serves various needs and demands.

**Task**: Develop a product or a range of products that underline the functionality and practicability of hemp and that helps to dispel concerns and prejudices concerning possible dangers.

## TEAM 6

**Situation:** The recent discussion about obesity, especially obese children, has led to the demand for healthier and less fattening food for children.

**Task:** The local **milk** industry wants your team to create and launch a product for children that is healthy and nutritious – but also liked by children.

**Some tips for your presentation:**

- Make sure that each member of your team takes on his/her part in the presentation.
- Think of ways to make your presentation informative <u>and</u> entertaining to attract your audience's attention.
- The product should take centre stage – not the people presenting it.
- If possible, try to provide samples of your product in order to give it to the audience/customer and allow them to try it.
- Use visuals and/or handouts to hold your audience's interest (OHP transparency, posters, etc.).
- Finally, thank your audience at the end of your presentation and tell them that they are welcome to ask further questions.

# Aspect 3: Action! – Advertising and sales in the movies

**Task 1: Improve your rhetorical skills and your advertising and marketing vocabulary.**

Das Strategy Sheet 12 (S. 23) sowie das Strategy Sheet 3 (S. 12) dienen zum einen der allgemeinen Wortschatzarbeit, zum anderen aber auch dem Erwerb eines vertiefenden Fachvokabulars im Bereich Medien und Werbung.

**Task 2: Discuss in class: which commercials and ads promoting sports equipment (e.g. sneakers, dresses, etc.) do you recall, and what is their specific message and target group?**

Die meisten Schülerinnen und Schüler sind in der Regel durch Fernsehen und Internet (YouTube) bestens über Produktwerbung, z. B. von Sportartikeln, informiert. Diese Redeanlässe können in Kleingruppen oder in Form eines „Kugellagers" diskutiert werden, sodass möglichst alle die Chance haben, sich zu äußern.

**Task 3: Watch the film *What women want* and find out about the development and composition of a commercial.**

Als vorbereitender Einstieg in die Analyse von Commercials dient das Info Sheet 13 (S. 24) sowie das Strategy Sheet 12 (S. 23). Mithilfe der „14 Tips" bekommen die Schülerinnen und Schüler eine erste Orientierung über die Methoden der Werbewelt. Das Info Sheet 13 kann, in Kombination mit dem auf DIN A3 hochkopierten Worksheet 16 (S. 28), zum Lesen als Hausaufgabe gegeben werden, mit der Zusatzaufgabe, sich Commercials unter Maßgabe dieses Kriterienkatalogs im Fernsehen anzuschauen und gute oder schlechte Beispiele in der nächsten Unterrichtsstunde zu thematisieren. Man kann Schüler auch bitten, Werbung auf DVD/Video aufzunehmen und mitzubringen. Interessant ist es, die Commercials (zunächst) ohne Ton anzuschauen und sich ganz auf die visuellen Impulse und Elemente zu konzentrieren. In Gruppen können die Schüler dann selber einen Werbetext zu den Bildmotiven entwerfen. Hier sind ganz verschiedene Lösungen denkbar – und erlaubt. Kreativität ist ausdrücklich erwünscht.
Der Film *What women want* (122 Minuten Laufzeit), von Regisseurin Nancy Meyers im Jahre 2000 gedreht, spielt in einer Werbeagentur in Chicago. Einer der Handlungsstränge beschreibt die Entwicklung einer Werbestrategie und Werbekampagne für NIKE Joggingschuhe für Frauen. Hier eignen sich besonders die (Film-)Kapitel 6, 12 und 16 für die Behandlung im Unterricht. Text 14 (S. 25) stellt Stills des Filmkapitels 16 bereit, anhand derer die Schüler ein Voice-over erstellen können (Worksheet 15, S. 26).

**Task 4: Exchange your personal experiences as consumers and become aware of legal and illegal sales practices.**

Zunächst können über die offene Fragestellung „Have you ever been tricked or duped by a salesman or in a shop?" die Erfahrungen der Schülerinnen und Schüler thematisiert werden. Mithilfe von Text 17 (S. 29), der Filmstills und Textauszüge aus dem Spielfilm *Tin men* bereitstellt, kann diese Thematik vertiefend diskutiert werden. In diesem Zusammenhang bietet sich auch die Thematisierung von *consumer protection* an. Die folgenden Websites bieten viele Informationen und könnten im Zuge einer Hausaufgabenrecherche sinnvoll eingesetzt werden: www.which.co.uk, www.asa.ora.uk (hier auch "The Cap Code" [= Committee of Advertising Practice]); die „which"-Seite zu detaillierten *consumer rights:* www.which.co.uk/reports_and_campaigns/consumer_rights/reports/your_rights/index.jsp.

**Task 5: Activate and practice your communication skills, and perform a role-play as "salesmen".**

In Form eines *role play* können die Schülerinnen und Schüler zum einen ihre erworbenen Kenntnisse, zum anderen ihre persönlichen Erfahrungen als Konsumenten anwenden und verarbeiten. Worksheet 18 (S. 30) stellt Material bereit *(role cards, useful expressions),* sodass in arbeitsteiliger Gruppen- oder Partnerarbeit ein Rollenspiel, das auch humorvoll oder ironisch sein darf, erarbeitet werden kann.

# Glossary of advertising terms

**to address sb** to say sth directly to sb

**advertisement/ad** a paid message in which the sponsor is identified

**to put an advertisement in a paper**

**advertising/agency/campaign/space/expert**

**A I D A** abbreviation of the formula (gain) **A**ttention (hold) **I**nterest (arouse) **D**esire (encourage to take) **A**ction

**to appeal to sb/appealing** attractive, interesting

**art director** an ad agency employee for designing and producing the artwork and layout

**article on/about sth** a piece of writing

**artificial** made or produced to copy sth natural; not real

**artificiality**

**at first sight; at first glance** when you first look at sth

**to attract sb/sb's attention**

**audiovisual presentation** a presentation involving both pictures and spoken words

**B & W** black and white ad

**bold; heavy-faced type** in a thick, dark type

**billboard/ billboard advertising** *große Reklamefläche*

**body copy** the main portion of the reading matter

**brand** the label by which a product is identified

**brand image (personality)** the pattern of feelings, ideas and images held by the public with regard to a specific brand

**brand loyalty** the tendency of customers to continue buying the same brand

**brochure** a booklet promoting a product or service

**capital letter** *Großbuchstabe*

**caption** text written underneath a picture to explain it

**client** customer

**clumsy** not well designed

**column** *Textspalte*

**competition/competitor** *Wettbewerb (-er)*

**consumer advertising** advertising of products sold to the general public

**to convince** make sb believe that sth is true by giving arguments

**conviction** strong opinion/belief

**to carry conviction** to be/sound convincing

**copy** any word or text material for publication, broadcast or production

**copywriter** a person who writes advertising

**to be creative, to work creatively**

**creativity**

**creative director** ad agency employee responsible for supervising the work of copywriters etc.

**direct response** specified advertising to reach individual customers (e. g. inquiry card system)

**editor** a person who is in charge of a newspaper etc.

**to evoke (interest in sth)** bring a feeling into your mind

**exaggerated** made to seem better/worse etc. than it is

**eye-catcher** *Blickfang*

**eye appeal** *Werbewirksamkeit*

**electronic media**

**field of vision** *Blickfeld*

**flashy** attracting attention by being bright, large etc.

**folding** sth that can be folded, e. g. a brochure

**front page** first page of a newspaper/magazine

**folder** a folded brochure

**four colour** artwork reproduced in full colour

**to glance at** to look quickly at sth

**to glamorize** to make sth bad appear attractive

**grouped style** *Blocksatz*

**hitting (making) the headlines**

**illustration (picture)**

**image** the public's perception of a firm or a product

**industrial advertising** advertising of industrial products

**jingle** music and lyrics used in a commercial

**label** *Etikett, Beschriftung*

**layout** arrangement of sth

**logo** the name and/or symbol of a company set in specially designed lettering

**market** population representing potential customers

**marketing/marketing communications**

**media**

**merchandising** activities designed to promote retail sales

**objective** what you want to accomplish

**passage, paragraph**

**to persuade sb** make sb agree to do/believe sth by giving them good reasons

**persuasive(ly)** being able to make sb do/believe sth

**persuasion**

**point of purchase** displays in stores designed to catch the customers' attention

**portfolio** presentation folder containing samples

**premium** a gift offered to potential customers

**prime time** peak viewing time, time when the greatest number of people are watching TV/listening to the radio

**print media**

**press**

**press release/news release** written news information mailed to the media

**promotion** activities used to encourage the purchase of a product

**psychographics** statistics relating to the personalities, attitudes and life styles of people

**public relations** activity of influencing the press so that they print stories that promote a company/product

**reply card** a self-addressed postcard

**research** careful study of a subject in order to discover new facts/information

**to skim a text** to read sth quickly/superficially

**to scan a text** to look quickly but not very carefully

**to seduce/seduction** *verführen/Verführung*

**slogan** a word or phrase that is easy to remember

**strategy** a plan to achieve a particular purpose

**subconscious(ly)** *unterbewusst*

**subheadline/-heading** title given to a part of an article

**supplement** an extra separate section that is sold with the newspaper/magazine

**sweepstakes** a sales promotion in which prizes are awarded to the customer

**tactics** strategy

**target group** a particular group of people the advertisement is aimed at

**trade advertising** advertising aimed at wholesalers, distributors and retailers rather than customers

**trademark** a name, symbol or design a company uses for its products and that cannot be used by anyone else

**two colour** ad printed in two colours, usually black and a second colour for effect

**unconscious(ly)** without being aware

# How to make TV commercials that sell – 14 tips by David Ogilvy

### 1 Brand identification

Research has demonstrated that a shocking percentage of viewers remember your commercial, but forget the name of your product. Here are two ways to register your brand name:

- Use the name within the first ten seconds. I have seen a brilliant commercial which repeated the brand name twenty times in 340 seconds, without irritating anyone.
- Play games with the name. Spell it. When you advertise a new product, you have to teach people its name on TV.

### 2 Show the package

Commercials which end by showing the package are more effective in changing brand preference than commercials which don't.

### 3 Food in motion

In commercials for food, the more appetizing you make it, the more you sell. It has been found that food in motion looks particularly appetizing. Show chocolate sauce in the act of being poured over your ice cream, or syrup over your pancakes.

### 4 Close-ups

It is a good thing to use close-ups when the product is the hero of your commercial. The closer you get on the candy bar, the more you make people's mouth water.

### 5 Open with the fire

You have only 3 seconds. If you grab attention in the first frame with a visual surprise, you stand a better chance of holding the viewer. People screen out a lot of commercials because they open with something dull. You know that great things are about to happen, but the viewer doesn't. When you advertise fire-extinguishers, open with the fire.

### 6 When you have nothing to say, sing it

There have been some successful commercials which sang the sales pitch, but jingles are below average in changing the brand preference. Research shows that this is neither a positive nor a negative factor. It does no harm and it does no measurable good. Do great preachers allow organists to play background music under their sermons? Do advertising agencies play background music under their pitch to prospective clients?

### 7 Sound effects

While music does not add to the selling power of commercials, sound effects such as sausages sizzling in a frying-pan – can make a positive difference.

### 8 Voice-over or on-camera?

Research shows that it is more difficult to hold your audience if you use voice-over. It's better to have the actors talk on camera.

### 9 Supers

It pays to reinforce your promise by setting it in type and superimposing it over the video, while your soundtrack speaks the words.

But make sure that the words in your supers are exactly the same as your spoken words. Any divergence confuses the viewer.

### 10 Avoid visual banality

If you want the viewer to pay attention to your commercial, show her something she has never seen before. The average American family has the television turned on for six hours a day, and is exposed to 30,000 commercials a year. Most of them slide off the memory like water off a duck's back. For this reason you should give commercials a touch of singularity, a visual burr that will stick on the viewer's mind.

### 11 Changes of scene

On the average, commercials with a plethora of short scenes are below average in changing a brand preference.

### 12 Mnemonics

This unpronounceable word is used to describe a visual device repeated over a long period. It can increase brand identification, and remind people of your promise.

### 13 Show the product in use

It pays to show the product being used, and, if possible, the end-result of using it. Show how your diapers (nappies) keep the baby dry. In a commercial for motor oil, show how the pistons look after 50,000 miles.

### 14 Everything is possible on TV

The technicians can produce anything you want. The limit is only your imagination.

adapted and compiled from David Ogilvy: Ogilvy on Advertising. New York, Vintage Books, 1985

# Film stills – The presentation scene in *What women want*

1

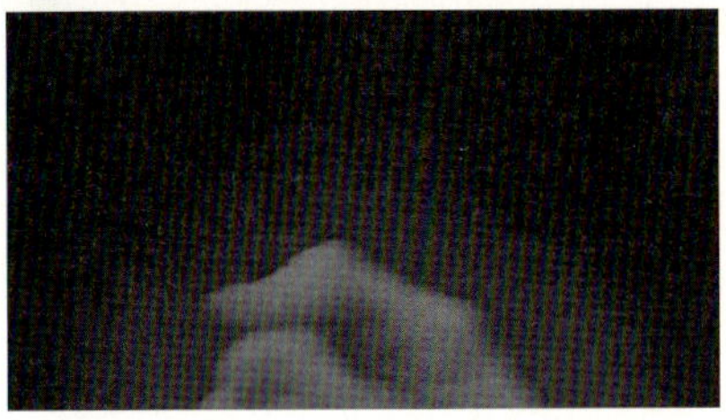

2

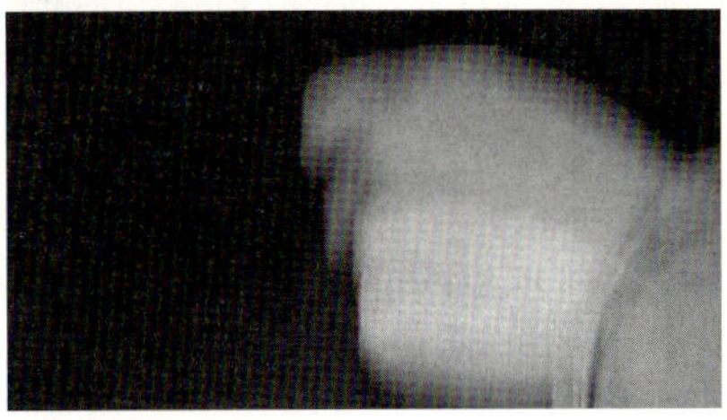

3

4

5

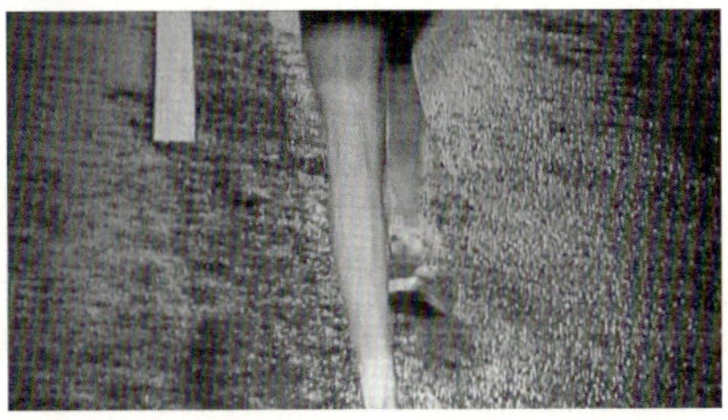

6

7

8

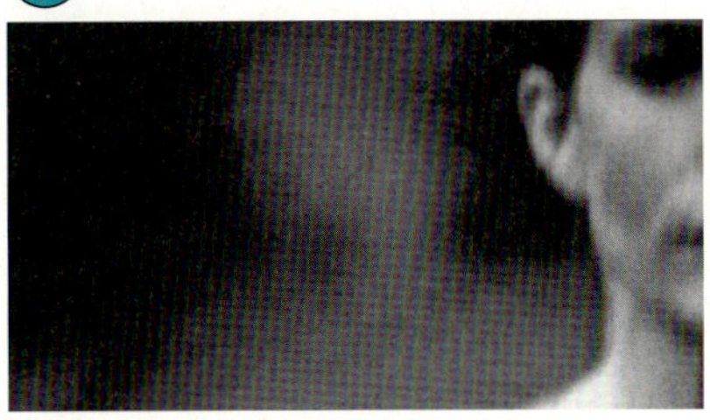

9

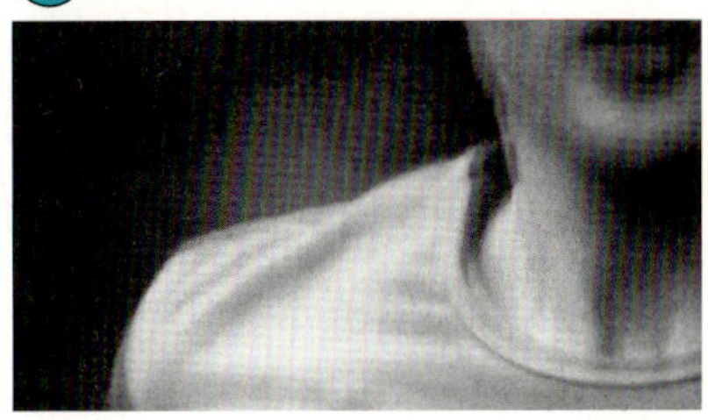

10

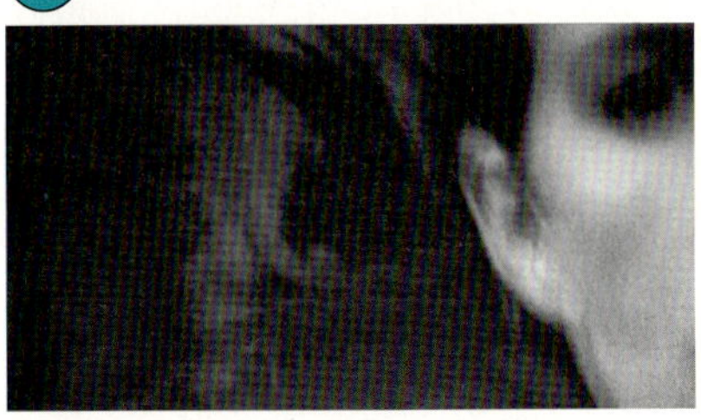

11

12

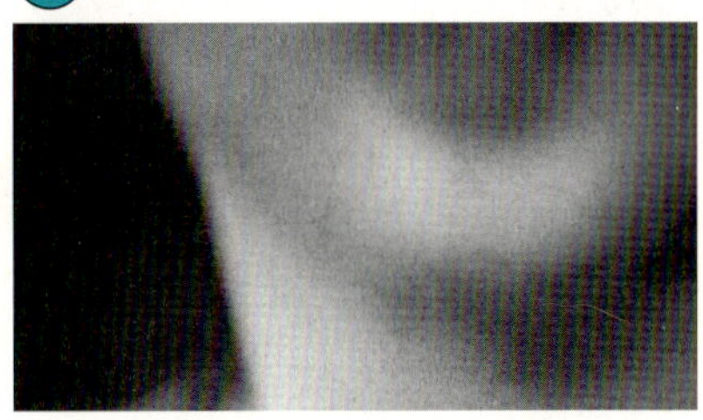

13

14

15

16

17

18

# Composing a voice-over for a NIKE commercial

In the presentation scene (1:29:24–1:30:15) the marketing director (Nick) presents the commercial, advertising sneakers for women, to his client (NIKE). Formulate a voice-over matching the given film stills from the commercial. What music/sound devices would you choose?

What is the effect of the commercial and its components on the viewer/customer? What is the implied/underlying message to the (female) customers? Who particularly is the target group?

| Voice-over text/sound | Image (film still) |
|---|---|
| | 1 dark background, focus on the back of a hand (fist) in upward motion |
| | 2 dark background, focus on the back of a fist/the wrist and the cuff of a grey sleeve |
| | 3 focus on the centre of a road marking, empty (wet) road going through a wooded area, the small image of a jogging woman wearing a T-shirt and shorts |
| | 4 focus is still on the centre of the road marking; woman is approaching |
| | 5 focus on the woman's naked legs from the back while she is running |
| | 6 focus on asphalt/street; only the woman's foot and a part of her calf can be seen |
| | 7 focus on wet asphalt and the centre of road marking; only a shadow can be seen |
| | 8 dark diffuse background, half of the woman's face; she is looking into the camera |
| | 9 woman is approaching the camera; woman's mouth, chin and her shoulder and neck can be partly seen |
| | 10 close-up of half of the woman's face |
| | 11 close-up of woman's face in full, blurred image |
| | 12 section of the woman's face in close-up, mouth, chin, very blurred image |
| | 13 focus on running woman approaching on the left (body: shoulder to thigh), dark road with centre marking |
| | 14 woman approaching, upper part of the body, dark road with centre marking |
| | 15 woman is passing by, half of her upper body; empty dark road with centre marking gets blurred |
| | 16 running woman from backwards, wet curved road with centre marking |
| | 17 wet curved road with centre marking; woman is disappearing, bottom right corner: NIKE logo |
| | 18 wet curved road with centre marking; woman has almost disappeared, bottom right corner: NIKE logo and slogan "No games. Just sports." |

| Voice-over text (Nick's presentation) | Sounds |
|---|---|
| You don't stand in front of a mirror before a run, and wonder what the road will think of your outfit.<br><br>You don't have to listen to its jokes and pretend they're funny in order to run on it.<br><br>It would not be easier to run if you dressed sexier.<br><br>The road doesn't notice if you're not wearing lipstick, does not care how old you are.<br><br>You do not feel uncomfortable because you make more money than the road.<br><br>And you can call on the road whenever you feel like it.<br><br>Whether it's been a day or even a couple of hours since your last date.<br><br>The only thing the road cares about is that you pay it a visit once in a while.<br><br>NIKE –<br><br>No games. Just sports. | **Music**<br>piano, strings, flutes;<br>melodious, cheerful, bright melody;<br>two rhythmical insertions;<br>relaxing, quiet<br><br>**Sounds**<br>the sound of the woman's feet on the road<br>the sound of the woman's breath/panting<br><br>(Note: You may combine film stills and voice-over texts/music/sounds due to your preferences.) |

**Effect on the viewer/customer**

- predominant feeling is confidence, trust, relaxation, silence, harmony
- running alone, the woman can feel free, she can be herself
- there is no need for styling, make-up and dressing-up
- running gives her a time off from work, business, stress, etc.
- running gives her time to think
- the woman is very natural and sporty
- as there is no one watching her she can look however she wants – even sweaty and casual
- there is no need to play games – and to pretend

**Implied/underlying message**

- if you wear NIKE sneakers, you will feel self-confident, balanced, strong
- if you wear NIKE sneakers, you can be yourself
- NIKE sneakers give their wearers the image of being sporty, successful, honest
- you can be yourself on the road – if you wear NIKE

**Target group**

- working women who need some time to relax from their job
- emancipated, self-confident women
- women who have a certain brand awareness and usually buy propriety articles/a certain trademark – and who can afford it

# Analysing and evaluating a commercial

| | | | | | | | |
|---|---|---|---|---|---|---|---|
| **Timing** | | | | | | | |
| **Field size** | | | | | | | |
| **Camera angle** | | | | | | | |
| **Camera movement** | | | | | | | |
| **Framing** | | | | | | | |
| **Montage/editing** | | | | | | | |
| **Sounds** | | | | | | | |
| **Lighting** | | | | | | | |
| **Special effects** | | | | | | | |
| **Text insertions/ voice over** | | | | | | | |
| **Function/ effect on the viewer/customer** | | | | | | | |

# *Tin men*: Salesmen's strategies and tricks – Legal or illegal?

1

In the front garden of a potential customer: "We're from LIFE magazine. We're doing a layout on the benefits of aluminum siding. The kind of 'before and after' presentation – special issue on home improvement. We already have a house that has aluminum siding that just looks like your house, except that it's ever so much more beautiful."

2

"I'll tell you what. Only on this sale, I'll throw in a garden hose for this sale."

3

To win the customer's confidence you drop a five-dollar bill an the ground like that. Then you go, "Oh, a five-dollar bill. Mr Blah-blah, would you like it back?" And two things happen: first thing he says, "It's not mine." That's when you say, "Must have been, because it's certainly not mine, sir." Or he says, "Thank you" and takes it. Either case he thinks you're an incredibly honest guy and you're in.

4

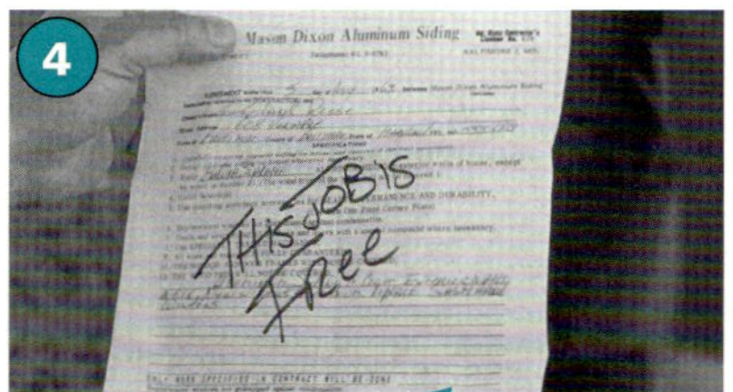


After this "sales job", a second tin man goes to the customer and says, "Mr Tilly is crazy, he had a nervous breakdown. But let's be honest. Nobody gives away a $4,200 worth of aluminum siding free. When I go to his boss and show him this contract, he'll be out of this business. He'll lose his home. His wife and kids will be thrown on the street. What do you say, we just sit down and try to work this out?"

5

"What do think if we made this house one of our factory showcase homes? We pick up same houses that are strategically located. We put up the aluminum siding and for every referral, I give you $400. – 100, 200, 300, 400. I'm giving you commission on two referrals before I even put a panel on the side of your house. That's how confident I feel."

6

"You approached the customer while he was cutting his front lawn, and told him that he had won an award and his house had been selected one of only sixteen homes in the state of Maryland for a free aluminum siding job. You suggested that for a nominal labor charge he would receive over $5,000 worth of aluminum siding. He then was charged $2,400 for labor which is about the average cost of an aluminum siding job. The job was sold under false terms."

# *Tin men* – Legal and illegal sales practices

Door-to-door sales

Ethically and legally incorrect ad

**1.** Look at the six film stills and the corresponding texts taken from the movie *Tin men*.
Which of the presented stills show illegal or unfair sales practices/unfair competition?
Why are these sales practices legal/illegal? What, in general, do you consider (il-)legal or (un-)fair sales practices?

**2.** Additionally, learn about consumer protection and consumer rights to support your assessment (www.which.co.uk and www.asa.org.uk).

**3.** Do a role play, one team playing the salesmen and the other team playing the target consumers. Possible scenarios can be: a door-to-door sales, telemarketing/telesales, a department store (e.g. furniture, an expensive dress, etc.).

- Before acting, you should work out a strategy to convince "your" customer.
- The students playing the customers should think about possible "defence" strategies in order not to get duped by the salesman/salesmen.

**Useful expressions**

- unfair competition
- to outsmart sb
- law against unfair practises/competition
- publicity ploy/gimmick
- to exert influence on sb
- to allude to the desire for sth
- suggestive character/power
- (lack of) succinctness and clarity
- to captivate the customer
- deception (of the customer)/to deceive sb
- unlawful practices
- to throw sb with a question
- to catch sb by surprise
- surprise tactics/surprise attack
- cheating/to cheat sb
- door-to-door sales
- the small print
- contrary to contract

**Useful expressions**

- **to pay sb compliments**
  Your ... is a very valuable piece of handicraft ...
  This is a very decorative ...
  This is a monument to your good taste ...
- **introducing yourself/your firm**
  I am a representative of ...
  I represent ...
- **showing concern/interest**
  Have you ever thought about ...
  Do you mind me asking ...
- **making suggestions**
  If I were you ... would ...
  Wouldn't it be a good idea to ...
  You wouldn't by any chance have ...
  Don't you think we should ...
- **approval of an idea**
  Oh, good. Excellent!
  Absolutely./Oh, definitely.

**1. The film stills:**

1. This sales job is illegal. → The aluminum siding was sold under false terms; the customer was cheated and the "hook", the promise of being on the front page of LIFE magazine was a lie.
2. This sales job is legal. → Offering some "extras"/gifts, provided the customer really gets them, is frequently practised.
3. The $5 bill: this is a legal trick to find something out about your target customer.
4. "This job is free": is an illegal job → the siding was sold under false terms; the customer was put under pressure; the salesmen lied to the consumer and appealed to his bad conscience.
5. $400 commission in advance: is legal → provided that the customer gets the money and the $400 aren't added later to the final price of the siding, the salesman can make the offer of becoming "a showcase home".
6. Making false promises to potential customers is illegal. → sales under false terms

**2. Consumer protection and consumer rights:**

In 1963, the year the film takes place, the state of **Maryland's Home Improvement Commission** instituted a "code of ethics", that also led to hearings as shown in the film. This code of ethics has undergone several changes and adaptations to protect the consumer legally, but also to provide legal certainty. The Home Improvement Commission's current website is: http://www.dsd.state.md.us/comar/idq_files/search.idq.

In **Great Britain** consumers can find information and advice from **"which?"**, a consumer advice institution that offers "legal advice from trusted lawyers, product testing reports, magazines, expert and unbiased information to help the consumer make the right choice and decision." This is comparable to Germany's *"Verbraucherberatung"* or *"Stiftung Warentest"*.

The **"Advertising Standards Authority"** ASA has stipulated rules that determine advertising practices, this is called the **CAP Code** (= Committee of Advertising Practice). These rules also stipulate honesty, truthfulness, decency and legality of marketing and advertising communications. Here are some examples:

1. "Marketers have primary responsibility for ensuring that their marketing communications are legal."
2. "Marketers should not exploit the credulity, lack of knowledge or inexperience of consumers."
3. "No marketing communication should mislead, or be likely to mislead, by inaccuracy, ambiguity, exaggeration, omission or otherwise."
4. "Marketers and publishers should make clear that advertisement features are advertisements, for example by heading them "advertisement feature".

# Aspect 4: "It's all illusion ..." – Marketing and sales in literature

**Task 1: Read the excerpt from Tennessee Williams' play *The last of my solid gold watches,* and find out how salesmanship and sales practices have changed over time.**

Der Textausschnitt (Text 19, S. 33 f.) beschreibt eine stereotype Situation, die Jugendliche vielleicht von ihren (Groß-)Eltern kennen. Der alte Salesman verharrt in der Vergangenheit, in Besserwisserei, die den jungen Mann nicht interessiert, vielleicht sogar abstößt oder belustigt. Er nimmt den alten Mann nicht ernst. Ergänzend zu den Aufgaben und Aktivitäten auf Worksheet 20 (S. 35) kann der Textausschnitt auch als *role-play* vorgelesen und gespielt werden. Für eine ergänzende und vertiefende Arbeit mit der Thematik – oder auch als Klausurtext – bieten sich weitere Textausschnitte aus folgenden Stücken/Büchern an:

1) Arthur Miller, *Death of a salesman* (Act I: dialogue Ben – Willy; Act II: dialogue Willy – Howard)

2) George Orwell, *Nineteen eighty-four* (Part I, Chapter 1: the Party slogans; Appendix: the principles and vocabulary of Newspeak)

3) William Shakespeare, *The merchant of Venice* (Act I, Scene 1: dialogue Antonio – Solanio; Act I, Scene 3: dialogue Bassanio – Shylock/Antonio – Shylock; Act III, Scenes 3 + 4)

4) Herbert Marcuse, *One-dimensional man* (The language of total administration, pp. 85–104)

**Task 2: Reflect on the purpose and effect of rhymes, as referred to in the extract from Aldous Huxley's utopian novel *Brave new world.***

Der vorliegende Ausschnitt (Worksheet 21, S. 37) verknüpft zwei wesentliche Aspekte: zum einen den Aspekt der Einflussnahme auf Menschen durch Sprache und Propaganda, der Kontrolle der Menschen durch den Staat sowie der entsprechenden gesellschaftspolitischen Mechanismen, zum anderen den Konflikt zwischen Gesellschaft und Individuum (Konformität – Individualität). Die Schülerinnen und Schüler sollen erkennen, welches Macht- und Manipulationsinstrument, das weit über den Aspekt des Verkaufens von Produkten hinausgeht, Werbung sein kann/ist. Ein schönes Experiment, um zu verdeutlichen, wie stark die Wirkung eines bestimmten Rhythmus' ist, ist, die Gruppe einen bestimmten Takt klatschen oder laufen zu lassen und dann ein oder zwei einzelne Schüler zu bitten, einen anderen Takt „gegen" die Gruppe zu klatschen/zu laufen und durchzuhalten – in der Regel gelingt dies nicht.

In Aspect 5 (Text 29, S. 48) wird die Thematik der Beeinflussung und Manipulation erneut aufgegriffen, hier jedoch mit Blick auf Politiker und (Wahl-)Slogans. An dieser Stelle sei auch auf ein interessantes Buch hingewiesen, einen Klassiker zum Thema Werbepsychologie: Vance Packard, *The Hidden Persuaders,* Great Britain 1957. Obwohl 50 Jahre alt, haben die darin beschriebenen und analysierten werbepsychologischen Grundprinzipien und Strategien immer noch Relevanz und sind in vielen Bereichen die Grundlage für das heutige Werbegeschäft.

**Task 3: Become aware of how the film industry makes use of product placement as a means of promotion, and read the excerpt from the screenplay *The Truman show.***

Am Beispiel dieser überdeutlichen Produktwerbung (Worksheet 22, S. 38) kann man die Schülerinnen und Schüler dafür sensibilisieren, in welchem Ausmaß und mit welcher Selbstverständlichkeit der Zuschauer durch Werbung beeinflusst wird. Im Rahmen einer gezielten (arbeitsteiligen) Beobachtungsaufgabe, z. B. als Hausaufgabe, können die Schüler untersuchen, in welchen Sendungen für welche Produkte und in welcher Weise und Häufigkeit direkt oder indirekt geworben wird. Dabei kommen sowohl Sportsendungen (Banden-/Trikotwerbung), Vorabendprogramm-„Soaps" als auch „Prime time"-Sendungen (Shows, Spielfilme, Krimis etc.) in Betracht. Interessant ist jeweils die Fragestellung, welche Zielgruppe in welcher Weise angesprochen wird. Welche Unterschiede bestehen zwischen den öffentlich-rechtlichen und den privaten Sendern? Worin unterscheidet sich Werbung im deutschen Fernsehen von Werbung bei CNN oder BBC? Die Ergebnisse könnten wahlweise auf Wandzeitungen präsentiert werden oder aber in Form einer Kugellagerübung diskutiert werden, sodass möglichst viele Schülerinnen und Schüler zum Zuge kommen.

Tennessee Williams

# The last of my solid gold watches

Tennessee Williams (1911–1983), born Thomas Lanier Williams III, was one of America's greatest dramatists. His writings were deeply influenced by his private life, his difficult childhood in a family dominated by his father, a travelling shoe salesman. The one-act play *The last of my solid gold watches (1947)* takes place in a hotel room in a Mississippi Delta town, and the protagonist, Mr. Charlie Colton, "is a legendary character, seventy-eight years old, ... superbly massive and with a kingly dignity of bearing".

**Mr. Charlie** (*ominously to himself*): Boom-boom-boom-boom-boom! Here comes th' parade! (*After some moments there comes a rap at the door.*) Come awn in! (*Harper, a salesman of thirty-five, enters. He has never known the "great days of the road" and there is no vestige of grandeur in his manner. He is lean and sallow and has a book of colored comics in his coat pocket.*)

**vestige** trace
**lean and sallow** thin and with an unhealthy yellow colour

**Harper:** How is the ole war-horse?

**Mr. Charlie** (*heartily*): Mighty fine an' dandy! How's the young squirrel?

**fine and' dandy** (*coll*) very good

**Harper:** Okay.

**Mr. Charlie:** That's the right answer! Step on in an' pour you'self a drink! Cigar?

**Harper** (*accepting both*): Thanks, Charlie. [...]

**Mr. Charlie:** *One* way – *another* way –! (*gravely*) Maybe you don't know it – but all of us ole-timers, Bob, are disappearin' *fast*! We all gotta quit the' road one time or another. Me, I reckon I'm pretty nearly the Last of th' Delta drummers!

**gravely** seriously

**Harper** (*restively squirming and glancing at his watch*): The Last of th' Delta drummers! How long you been on th' road?

**restively squirming** impatiently moving about

**Mr. Charlie:** Fawty-six yeahs in Mahch!

**Harper:** I don't believe yuh.

**Mr. Charlie:** Why would I tell you a lie about something like that? No, suh, I want you t' know – I want you t' know – Hmmm. ... I lost a mighty good customer this week.

**Harper** (*with total disinterest, adjusting the crotch of his trousers*): How's that, Charlie?

**crotch** *Schritt*

**Mr. Charlie** (*grimly*): Ole Ben Summers – Friar's Point, Mississippi ... pour himself a drink at the Cotton Planter's Cotillion!

**grimly** seriously
**cotillion** a formal ball

**Harper:** Ain't that terrible, though! What was the trouble?

**Mr. Charlie:** Mortality, that was the trouble! Some people think that millions now living are never going to *die*. I don't think that – I think it's a misapprehension not borne out by the facts! We go like flies when we come to the end of the summer ... And who is going to prevent it! (*He nods gravely.*) The road is changed. The shoe industry is changed. These times are – revolution! (*He rises and moves to the window.*) I don't like the way that it looks. You can take it from me – the world that I used to know – the world that this boy's father used t'know – the world we belonged to, us old time warhorses! – is slipping and sliding away from under shoes. Who is going to prevent it? The ALL-LEATHER slogan don't sell shoes any more. The stuff that a shoe's made of is not what's going to sell it any more! No! STYLE! SMARTNESS! APPEARANCE! That's what counts with the modern shoe-purchaser, Bob! But

**mortality** *Sterblichkeit*
**misapprehension** a wrong idea about sth

try an' tell your style department that. Why, I remember the time when all I had to do was lay out my samples down there in the lobby. Open up my order-book an' write out orders until my fingers *ached*! A *sales-talk* was not *necessary*. A store was a place where people sold merchandise and to sell merchandise the retail-dealer had to obtain it from the wholesale manufacturer, Bob! Where they get merchandise now I do not pretend to know. But it don't look like they buy it from wholesale dealers! Out of the air – I guess it materializes! Or maybe stores don't *sell* stuff any more! Maybe I'm living in a world of illusion! I recognize that possibility, too!

**Harper** (*casually, removing the comic paper from his pocket*): Yep – yep. You must have witnessed some changes.

**Mr. Charlie:** Changes? A mild expression. Young man – I have witnessed – a REVOLUTION! (*Harper has opened his comic paper but Mr. Charlie doesn't notice, for now his peroration is really addressed to himself.*) Yes, a *revolution*! The atmosphere that *I breathe* is not the same! Ah, well – I'm an old war-horse. (*He opens his coat and lifts the multiple golden chains from his vest. An amazing number of watches rise into view. Softly, proudly he speaks.*) Looky here, young fellow! You ever seen a man with this many watches? How did I *acquire* this many time-pieces? (*Harper has seen them before. He glances above the comic sheet with affected amazement.*) At everyone of the annual sales conventions of the Cosmopolitan Shoe Company in St. Louis a seventeen-jewel, solid-gold, Swiss-movement Hamilton watch is presented to the ranking salesman of the year! Fifteen of those watches have been awarded to me! I think that represents *something*! I think that's something in the way of achievement! ... Don't *you*?

**Harper:** Yes, *siree*! You bet, I *do*, Mistuh Charlie! (*He chuckles at a remark in the comic sheet. Mr. Charlie slicks out his lips with a grunt of disgust and snatches the comic sheet from the young man s hands.*)

**Mr. Charlie:** Young man – I'm talkin' to *you*, I'm talkin' for your *benefit*. And I expect the courtesy of your attention until I am through! I may be an old war-horse. I may have received – the last of my solid gold watches ... But just the same – good manners are still a part of the road's tradition. [...] My point is this: the ALL-LEATHER slogan is not what sells any more – not in shoes and not in humanity, neither! The emphasis isn't on quality. Production, production, yes! But out of inferior goods! *Ersatz* – that's what they're making 'em out of!

**Harper** (*getting up*): That's your opinion because you belong to the past.

**Mr. Charlie** (*furiously*): A piece of impertinence, young man! I expect to be accorded a certain amount of respect by whippersnappers like you!

**Harper:** Hold on, Charlie.

**Mr. Charlie:** I belong to – tradition. I am a *legend*. Known from one end of the Delta to the other Form the Peabody Hotel in Memphis to Catfish Row in Vicksburg. *Mistuh Charlie* – Mistuh Charlie! Who knows *you*? What do *you* represent? A line of goods of doubtful value, some kike concern in the East! Get out of my room! I'd rather play solitaire, than poker with men who're no more solid characters than the jacks in the deck! (*He opens the door for the young salesman who shrugs and steps out with alacrity. Then he slams the door shut and breathes heavily.* [...]) This room was like a *throne*-room.



**retail-dealer** *Einzelhändler*

**wholesale dealer** *Großhändler, Grossist*

**peroration** a long speech that is not very interesting

**time-piece** watch

**affected** not natural or sincere

**ranking** having a high or highest rank

**to chuckle** to laugh quietly

**benefit** good

**courtesy** politeness

**inferior** not good

**impertinence** *Unverschämtheit*

**to accord** to give

**whippersnapper** *junger Spund*

**kike** (*sl*) Jew

**jack** a playing card (*Bube*)

**to shrug** to raise and then drop your shoulders to show that you do not care

**alacrity** enthusiasm

Tennessee Williams

# The last of my solid gold watches

## Before reading

Published in 1946, the play contains various references to *President Roosevelt* and the politics of the *New Deal* and its consequences.

**1.** Learn about the historical background of the given scene.

**2.** Which social, political and economic changes in the U.S. did this era bring forth?

**3.** When (especially old) people talk about "the good old times", they are often very subjective, sentimentalize events and/or lament the present (bad) situation. They usually see their heydays through rose-tinted glasses whereas nowadays "everything's going downhill".
Work in groups of 3–4 students, discuss and collect statements your parents or grandparents frequently make on:
a) "the good old times" and
b) the current situation (economy, rising prices, behaviour of (young) people, etc.)

- How do you/young people/people in general react to this kind of complaining?
- Do you think that there is a grain of truth in these laments?

## While reading

**1.** How is the "old" and the "new" world (re-)presented in the given extract?
What is Mr. Charlie's attitude towards these changes?

**2.** What references to death and decay are employed in the scene that convey its melancholic atmosphere and reminiscences of a time/past long passed?

**3.** In what way does the playwright show sympathy with Mr. Charlie and his distress – and how does he evoke the reader's sympathy for Mr. Charlie?

**4.** Mr. Charlie says that he "has witnessed a revolution" during the forty-six years of his salesmanship. What revolutionary changes does he mean/refer to?
Think of similar (revolutionary, dramatic) changes that have taken place in the last fifty years (in Germany/Europe/globally).

## After reading

**1.** "The ALL-LEATHER slogan don't sell shoes anymore ... STYLE! SMARTNESS! APPEARANCE! That's what counts ... The emphasis isn't on quality ... *Ersatz* ..." Compare Mr. Charlie's statement to marketing techniques and strategies in today's globalized economy. To what extent are modern products only "tinsel" and fake – and does style and appearance count?

**2.** Form groups and work creatively with the text.
Shift the perspective of the given extract to a different time, place or/and culture. Take care that the basic messages are expressed and that the plot basically doesn't change.
Example: Depression → today's world/globalization

- What can an employee/salesman/worker complain about in the globalised world?
- You can change the setting as well, e.g. sweatshop in China, village in Africa/India, etc.

**3.** Read Arthur Miller's play *Death of a salesman* or watch (scenes of) the film. Compare Willie Loman with Mr. Charlie, and Miller's stance on the change of values, society and people's way of dealing with loss and frustration to Williams' view.

## Before reading

**1. President Franklin D. Roosevelt ("FDR", 1933–1945):** democratic politician, a cheerful man who gave Americans confidence; the only president to be elected four times; suffered from polio and could hardly walk without help; his illness made him a more compassionate person and his political actions reflect that; as a governor he attempted to help underprivileged people (unemployment insurance, child labour laws, old-age pensions); after his election Roosevelt immediately started governmental reforms

**2. The Great Depression and the New Deal:** After the stock market crash in 1929, the U.S. economy continued to decline, millions of people were out of work; when Roosevelt started political reforms he brought forth the greatest change ever in the political and economic life of the nation; the Social Security Act of 1935 set up a system of unemployment insurance and old-age pension; the Agricultural Adjustment Act (AAA) aimed at pushing agricultural prices up by reducing the amount of crops produced; FDR's New Deal reforms changed the face of American politics, proving that the central government could serve as a source of social and economic change; after FDR's death, in April 1945, the U.S. economy was booming again and die U.S. the world's most prosperous and powerful nation

## While reading

**1.**

| Old world | New world | Mr. Charlie's attitude |
|---|---|---|
| • Mr. Charlie (superbly massive ... kingly dignity)<br>• us ole-timers ... disappearin'<br>• last of the old Delta Drummers<br>• forty-six years on the road<br>• mortality ... that's the trouble<br>• the world we belonged to ... is slipping and sliding away<br>• we go like flies<br>• the all-leather slogan don't sell shoes anymore<br>• a sales-talk was not necessary<br>• an old war-horse<br>• salesman of the year<br>• fifteen watches ... awarded to me<br>• humanity, quality, solidity<br>• tradition, respect, manners<br>• like a throne-room<br>• shouting, laughing, hilarity | • Harper (lean and sallow)<br>• reads comics<br>• restively squirming, glancing at his watch<br>• has never known the great days of the road<br>• I don't believe you (→distrust)<br>• total disinterest (→ignorance)<br>• adjusting the crotch of his trousers (→lack of manners)<br>• the shoe industry's changed<br>• style, smartness, appearance<br>• stores don't sell stuff anymore (→supermarkets)<br>• inferior goods ... Ersatz<br>• a line of goods of doubtful value ... kike concern ... jacks | • the young squirrel<br>• misapprehension ... not born out by the facts<br>• a revolution<br>• a grunt of disgust<br>• expects the courtesy of attention<br>• a piece of impertinence<br>• whippersnappers like you<br>• I am a legend<br>• men who're jacks in the deck<br>• I'd rather play solitaire than poker with jacks<br>• commanding respect<br>• living in a world of illusion |

**2.** Allusions and references to mortality, death and decay can be found throughout the whole scene: l. 11 gravely; l. 12 disappearin' fast, quit the' road; l. 26 mortality; l. 28 we go like flies … the end of the summer; l. 29 nods gravely; l. 43 out of the air; l. 65 the <u>last</u> of my …; l. 81 this room <u>was</u> like …

**3.** Despite of his "grunting", grumbling and moaning, there are positive character traits employed to characterise Mr. Charlie (<u>superbly</u> massive, <u>kingly</u> dignity) as an impressive man. Additionally, the reader's sympathy is evoked by referring to his loneliness (all his friends are dead, Ole Ben Summers …) and his obvious isolation. By contrasting Mr. Charlie's dignity and values to Harper's rather negative character traits and manners (see table above) this effect is emphasized even more.

**4.** Possible references to the technical revolution (Internet, exploration of space, genetic engineering), (end of) Cold War, climate change, terrorism, etc.

Aldous Huxley

# *Brave new world* – On the use of rhymes in moral propaganda and advertising

At their first meeting after the estrangement, Bernard poured out the tale of his miseries and accepted consolation. It was not till some days later that he learned, to his surprise and with the twinge of shame, that he was not the only one who had been in trouble. Helmholtz had also come into conflict with Authority.

"It was over some rhymes," he explained. "I was giving my usual course of Advanced Emotional Engineering for Third Year Students. Twelve lectures, of which the seventh is about rhymes. "On the Use of Rhymes in Moral Propaganda and Advertisement," to be precise. I always illustrate my lecture with a lot of technical examples. This time I thought I'd give them one I'd just written myself. Pure madness, of course; but I couldn't resist it." He laughed. "I was curious to see what their reactions would be. Besides," he added more gravely, "I wanted to do a bit of propaganda; I was trying to engineer them into feeling as I'd felt when I wrote the rhymes. Ford!" He laughed again. "What an outcry there was! The Principal had me up and threatened to hand me to immediate sack. I'm a marked man."

"But what were your rhymes?" Bernard asked.

"They were about being alone."

Bernard's eyebrows went up.

"I'll recite them to you, if you like." And Helmholtz began:

"Yesterday's committee,
Sticks, but a broken drum,
Midnight in the City,
Flutes in a vacuum,
Shut lips, sleeping faces,
Every stopped machine,
The dumb and littered places
Where crowds have been –
All silences rejoice,
Weep (loudly or low),
Speak – but with the voice
Of whom I do not know.

Absence, say, of Susan's,
Absence of Egeria's
Arms and respective bosoms,
Lips and, ah, posteriors,
Slowly form a presence;
Whose? And I ask, of what
So absurd an essence,
That something, which is not,
Nevertheless should populate
Empty night more solidly
Than that which we copulate,
Why should it seem so squalidly?

Well, I gave them that as an example, and they reported me to the Principal."

"I'm not surprised," said Bernard. "It's flatly against all their sleep-teaching. Remember, they've just had at least a quarter of a million warnings against solitude."

"I know. [...] I feel as though I were just beginning to have something to write about. As though I were beginning to be able to use that power I feel I've got inside me – that extra, latent power."

Aldous Huxley: Brave New World. London, Flamingo Books, 1994, pp. 163–165

**twinge** a sudden short feeling of pain

**Ford** instead of using "Lord"; in memory of Henry Ford (1863–1947), inventor of the assembly line

**sack** *(BrE infml)* being told by your employer that you can no longer work for the company

**Egeria** girl named after the mythical adviser of Numa, legendary second king of Rome

**posterior** part of your body that you sit on; your bottom

**to rejoice** to express great happiness about sth

**squalid** here: involving low moral standards or dishonest behaviour

**1.** Examine the rhyming words in the poem. What emotions do they appeal to – and which "moral" do they advertise?

**2.** Why can "being alone" (l. 16) be bad or dangerous? Do you recall any ads/commercials that promote "the joy of being alone"?

# *The Truman Show* – product placement and promotion

*Meryl joins Truman at the kitchen table. Truman applauds ironically.*

**Meryl:** Let me get you some help, Truman. You're not well.

**Truman** (*ignoring her medical advice*): Why do you want to have a child with me? You can't stand me.

**Meryl:** That's not true.

*Meryl picks up a package and holds it to camera.*

**Meryl:** Why don't I make you some of this new Mococoa Drink? All natural. Cocoa beans from the upper slopes of Mount Nicaragua. No artificial sweeteners –

**Truman** (*incredulous*): What the hell are you talking about?!

**Meryl:** I've tasted other cocoas. This is the best.

*Truman rises frorn the table and backs her around the room.*

**Truman:** What the hell has that got to do with anything? Tell me what's happening?!

**Meryl** (*frightened but remaining poised*): You're having a nervous breakdown, that's what's happening.

**Truman** (*backing her up against the kitchen bench*): You're part of this, aren't you?!

*Meryl grabs the "Chef's-Mate" from the counter to protect herself. She points the potato peeler at him.*

**Meryl:** Truman, you're scaring me!

*Truman looks into her eyes and, with surprising swiftness, grabs her wrist and disarms her.*

**Truman:** No, you're scaring me, Meryl!

*Truman grabs Meryl and turns the Chef's-Mate on her. He stares wildly about him.*

**Truman:** Stop this now. I'll do it. I swear.

**Meryl:** Do something ...

*Upon hearing her remark, Truman's eyes widen. Sensing that she too is addressing a third person, he jerks her head around to read her face.*

**Truman** (*wild-eyed*): Who were you talking to?!

Andrew Niccol: The Truman Show. The Shooting Script. London, Nick Hern Books, 1998

Explain in what way product placement incites viewers to buy a certain product.
Which TV programmes/series/soaps you know employ direct/indirect product placement?

**1. Rhyming words**

| | |
|---|---|
| (yesterday's) committee – (midnight) city<br>(broken) drum – vacuum<br>(sleeping) faces – (littered) places | negative images (emptiness, dirt, tiredness) ↓ |
| (silences) rejoice – voice<br>(weep) low – (do not) know | praise of silence, solitude, emotions ↓ |
| [absence of ...]<br>Susan's – bosoms<br>Egeria's – posteriors<br><br>presence – essence<br>populate – copulate<br>solidly – squalidly | sexual allusions/images (emotion/lust/desire)<br>→ longing for/imagination of something that is missing |

- (Unanswered) question: why should solitude ("empty night") seem morally bad or dishonest ("squalid")?
- Asking (unwanted) questions can be dangerous.
- As moral principles are a matter of definition, they vary due in historical and social background – and are therefore often subject to discussion and interpretation/protest.
- Function of rhymes: they can be easily remembered; rhymes/rhythms appeal to people's emotions (rhythm → heart-beat, music, songs ...); rhymes/rhythms can cheer people up or calm them down.

**2.** a) As the novel *Brave new* world exemplifies the situation of people living in a totalitarian regime, it also reveals how the state controls the people (masses); thus, being alone consequently means evading society, possibly in order to escape control. Somebody who always keeps very much to himself, is often considered an opponent of the political system, a danger, an enemy – and therefore has to be punished. This understanding also matches the basic idea of George Orwell's novel *Nineteen eighty-four* in which the protagonist attempts to escape the permanent control of "Big Brother".

b) Ads or commercials that promote "the joy of being alone" usually emphasize solitude as a hideaway from everyday stress and duties, e.g. the "NIKE commercial" (Text 14, p. 25), the "Jever Pilsener" commercial and some commercials promoting cars underline the feeling/expression of individualism, self-determination and relaxation in contrast to a stressful job etc. These commercials are in contrast to the more commonly used appeal to the masses or the herd instinct or peer pressure (being together = fun/ excitement/happiness, etc. ↔ solitude = isolation/sadness/boredom, etc.).

---



Product placement appeals to people's subconscious; while watching a film/soap/football game, etc. they are (more or less permanently) exposed to certain products and their messages, usually without becoming aware of it. Companies pay enormous sums of money to broadcasters to promote certain products (in a more or less subtle way), which has led to various legal proceedings. Of course, the legal position varies from country to country – (see: www.usatoday.com/life/television/news/2006-09-19-product-integration_x.htm and www.out-law.com/page-6455) but product placement has become a major source of income for broadcasters to finance their productions.

# Aspect 5: No limits at all? – How advertising influences people

**Task 1: Experience how advertising strategies change in order to meet new trends and changing attitudes.**

Die Schülerinnen und Schüler sollen hier erfahren, dass nicht nur Industrie und Werbung versuchen, Verbraucherverhalten in ihrem Sinne zu beeinflussen, sondern dass auch Verbraucher mit ihren geänderten Bedürfnissen, z. B. aufgrund demographischen Wandels, wiederum das Angebot und die Werbestrategien verändern. Werbeanzeigen wie Text 23, S. 41 und der nachfolgende Text 24, S. 42 machen dieses sichtbar. Die entsprechende Transparency 1 kann den Schülerinnen und Schülern dabei zunächst als stummer Impuls dargeboten werden, anschließend können die Erkenntnisse mithilfe von Text 24 vertieft und kritisch hinterfragt werden. Worksheet 25, S. 43 eignet sich dann zur Übertragung und Vertiefung.

**Task 2: Consumer protection versus freedom of advertising: discuss the pros and cons.**

Die Schülerinnen und Schüler sollten hier für die Möglichkeiten einer 'Anti-Werbung', den Grenzen, die man Werbung selbst in ihrem Wahrheitsgehalt setzen sollte, und des Verbraucherschutzes, der im weitesten Sinne auch ein vollständiges Werbeverbot beinhalten könnte, sensibilisiert werden. Dazu eignen sich besonders die Aufgaben 'Honesty and truth ... auf Worksheet 25, S. 43.

**Task 3: Analyse how Hollywood celebrities are used to promote cars, and design your own commercial starring famous actors and VIPs.**

Der Wiedererkennungswert eines Produktes und das Anlocken von Käufern wird in der Werbung häufig mithilfe bekannter Persönlichkeiten aus Sport, Kultur oder Politik bewerkstelligt. Dieses sollte anhand der Aufgaben auf Worksheet 26, S. 45 erarbeitet werden. Worksheet 16, S. 28 (*Analysis of commercials*) sollte jedoch vorher bearbeitet worden sein. Zur Gestaltung von eigenen Commercials ist der Einsatz des Programms „Power-DVD" sinnvoll: es besitzt die Funktion „Snapshots", mit deren Hilfe sich gezielte Filmstills auswählen und dann in Word übertragen, arrangieren und bearbeiten lassen. Über einzelne Filmstills lässt sich so ein eigenes Commercial gezielt „zusammenschneiden".

**Task 4: Learn about marketing campaigns that went wrong and came to nothing.**

Nicht jede Werbekampagne erreicht das definierte Ziel. Den Schülerinnen und Schülern kann hier mit Text 27, S. 46 und Text 28, S. 47 vermittelt werden, dass der Vampir-Effekt, so lustig er zunächst auch scheinen mag, Kapital vernichtet und erwartete Nachfrage, die ja auch Investitionen voraussetzt, Firmen durchaus finanziell in eine Schieflage bringen kann. Andererseits kann neue Nachfrage generiert werden. Auf der folgenden Website kann man das „Wackel-Elvis Commercial" kostenfrei herunterladen: www.videos.scores.de/elvis_audi_werbung.shtml.

**Task 5: Become aware of how politics create public images and adjust truth/reality to necessities. Do political campaigning yourself and create catchy slogans.**

Anhand dieser Aufgaben können zentralabiturrelevante Themen (z. B. Utopia and dystopia – George Orwell, *1984*, *America then and now*) wiederholt oder aufgearbeitet werden. Der kreative Ansatz, eine eigene Wahlkampagne zu planen und an Wünschen der zu erreichenden Wähler auszurichten, das eigene Image dementsprechend zu kreieren, sensibilisiert die Schülerinnen und Schüler für PR-Tricks und hilft bei der Analyse der politischen Persuasion. Hierzu kann Text 29, S. 48 und das Strategy Sheet 30, S. 49 bearbeitet werden (s.a. Transparency 2). Weiteres Hintergrundmaterial zu *slogans* und *political campaigns* bieten u. a. die folgenden Websites: http://en.wikipedia.org/wiki/Public_relations, http://en.wikipedia.org/wiki/Slogan. Die Thematik bietet darüberhinaus auch lohnende Themen für Facharbeiten. Für den Einsatz im Unterricht oder ergänzende Referate eignen sich auch die folgenden Filme (oder Sequenzen daraus):
1. *The candidate* (1972, Robert Redford); 2. *Wag the dog* (1997, Dustin Hoffman); 3. *American political commercials* (1999); 4. *Welcome to Mooseport* (2003, Gene Hackman); 5. *Thank you for smoking* (2005, Aaron Eckhart).

# Advertising campaigns: Changing trends and changing strategies

Toyota 2000GT

Power ...

... versus ecology

Anorexic models ...

... versus "real women"

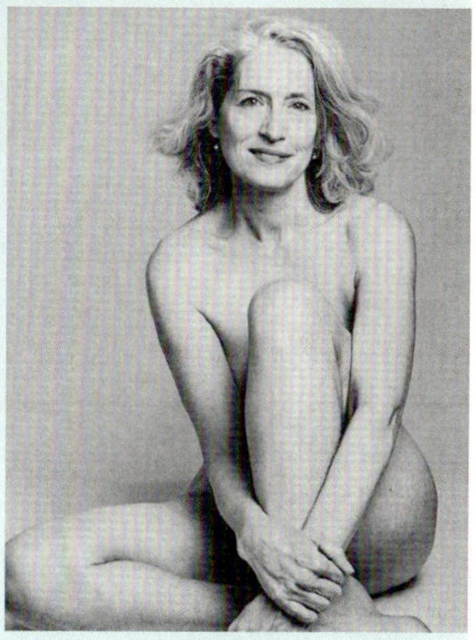

"Anti-age"... versus "Pro-age"

Supersize ...

... versus "balanced diet"

# Wrinkles in living color – Dove sells a new line of beauty products by telling women that aging is O.K.

Are you Anti-Age or Pro-Age?

A bare shoulder flashes on the screen to the riffs of a flamenco guitar. A feminine hand on an unclothed waist follows, and the gorgeous face of a dark-haired woman appears with – yikes! – all her wrinkles in living color. The camera pulls back, and – double yikes! – she's naked. Next, a grinning full-figured woman with silver-streaked hair. Then comes an age-spotted shoulder. Finally, a long-legged beauty with cropped grey hair and – egads! – a lined neck and a furrowed brow poses in the buff, save for a pair of dangling earrings and a cuff bracelet.

These stunning images, shot by celebrity photographer Annie Leibovitz, are the centrepiece of a counterintuitive new ad campaign by the maker of Dove soap to promote its latest line of beauty products. In its first global launch ever, Dove hopes to attract the 40 million or so baby-boomer women in the wrinkle-war zone with a provocative twist: instead of demonizing wrinkles with "anti-aging" products, Dove celebrates them and calls its new line Pro Age. For the Anglo-Dutch consumer giant Unilever, Dove's $52 billion parent company, the stakes are high: sales in 2006 grew just 4%. [...]

"We live in an anti-age culture, no question," says Susie Orbach, a British psycho-analyst and author, who helped conduct a Unilever/Dove-sponsored beauty survey of women in nine countries. Anti-aging skin care accounts for nearly $13 billion in sales worldwide, according to Euromonitor, and it is on the way to $17 billion by 2010. Dove's study found that 91% of women over 50 feel they're not represented realistically in the media. "They feel invisible," Orbach says.

That's one thing the women in Dove's Pro Age campaign certainly are not. It builds on the success of Dove's "Campaign for Real Beauty", a series of ads with full-figured women that earned it every marketer's dream – an appearance on *The Oprah Winfrey Show*. The Pro Age television, print and Web ads (one deemed too racy for broadcast TV) feature real women, not models, all age 50 or over. "We want to widen the stereotypical view of beauty", says Dove's U.S. marketing director, Kathy O'Brien, 42. [...] To win older women over, Dove puts a positive spin on the unhappy moment when a woman buys her first jar of anti-wrinkle cream. "The concept is linguistically brilliant", says Cheryl Swanson, a managing partner at Toniq, a brand-strategy firm in New York City. "Skin care has typically been about fighting back – age defying. It's been almost warrior-like. Take a stance against this natural thing that's happening to you. This is different." The strategy tells women, implicitly, that they can look better without trying too hard. [...] Last spring the company [L'Oréal] signed the actress Diane Keaton, 61, to be the spokeswoman for Age Perfect Pro-Calcium skin cream, a product for "mature, fragile skin."

Dove's campaign goes much further in rejecting the conventions of beauty marketing. So far, in fact, that some of the posts on Dove's own website reacting to the new ads have been critical of the reveal-all. "The public is not ready to see that", one post noted; another called the ads "a little too vivid". What many think is beautiful and refreshing, others find jarring and offensive. [...] When it comes to what's inside the bottle, Dove's Pro Age products are much like other anti-aging products. The key ingredient, alpha hydroxy acid, is found in many anti-aging products and helps exfoliate the top layers of skin to reveal fresher skin underneath.

TIME, April 16, 2007, pp. 39f.

**Gray Is the New Blond.** Botox may reign, but a few of Hollywood's silver foxes are proudly wearing the signs of their age and experience.

**Jamie Lee Curtis:** She once posed in More magazine without makeup.

**Diane Keaton:** The actress did a nude scene in a film at age 57.

**Helen Mirren:** The 60 year old actress has fan sites and an Oscar.

**Carmen Dell-Orefice:** Silver hair is the trademark of the actress and model.

# Advertising reacts to consumer demands and new trends

### Advertising reacts to consumer demands and new trends

**1.** You are CEO for one of the large advertising agencies and you see that the ageing society has a great demand for utensils and items that help the elderly. On the other hand older people don't want to appear to be frail and disabled. Start an advertising campaign promoting these products generating a positive image of the elderly.

**2.** Great demand for energy at last induces car producers like BMW or VW to rethink their concepts and start promoting energy saving, environmental friendly cars. Your clients, however, want speed instead. Create a commercial where you point out that buying your brand makes the idea of speedy cars redundant.

"This no-nonsense approach appeals to a new breed of consumer who wants to be dealt with honesty."

"If you're risking cancer, shouldn't your cigarette deliver real flavour? Shouldn't something that might make you die, really taste great?"

"Stop pretending. If you look like this, then you're fat. In fact, you're a fat slob. Admit it. Then do something about it.
Want to stop sweating on relatively cool days? Get to a phone. Call Vita Flex toll-free now. If you call now, we'll send you a free plant."

Excerpts (voice-overs) from the film *Crazy People*, © Paramount Pictures 1990

### Honesty and truth in advertising – do consumers want to be told the truth?

**1.** Imagine: You are fat or a smoker. You write a letter to the company whose product is advertised and state your reaction to the ad. (You can use words like revealing, honest, amusing, outrageous, shocking, insulting, etc.)

**2.** Imagine: You are a travel agent. You have experienced that everything in your holiday was just the opposite of what the advertisement had promised.
Now two customers come to you and ask you whether you can recommend travelling to India, what your personal experience was, etc. Do you tell them the truth or would you rather make sure that they book the flight and hotel?
a) Do a role play.
b) Each student of the group should state the feelings she/he had in the situation.

**3.** **Activity:** Discuss the pros and cons of anti-ads/the renunciation of ads in a debate. Create anti-ads yourself that deal with smoking/alcohol/drugs/wasting energy, etc.

### Advertising reacts to consumer demands and new trends

**1.** Students should collect ideas about what utensils, items and help seniors need. Example: If someone has difficulties with poor eyesight, he might want a larger screen display or sth that might help him find the way (clothes, canes or hearing aids). With the help of the Internet the students can find out that worldwide the problems of ageing societies are on the increase. Exploding costs make it a necessity people to be able to care for themselves as long as possible. To avoid seniors feeling insulted by being offered such products students can show them as self-confidently handling disabilities, as clever because they have found solutions to their problem and as demanding the best quality.

**2.** Students could create such an advert by looking at the rising global demand for energy especially by the new great global players like China and India as well as the threats of global warming. They should also look at the target group. Who can afford such a car? Why would they want speed? What can replace the wish to race the car?

### Honesty and truth in advertising – do consumers want to be told the truth?

**1.** Students could point out the difference between truth and insult. Although there is a demand for information that is partly satisfied by consumer protection boards like 'Stiftung Warentest' or 'Which' in England they can emphasise that adverts shouldn't be misleading or tell lies on purpose. Being too blunt, however, could not only make consumers **not** buy the product, it could also lead to distress (e.g. when you are obese and suffering from an eating disorder) and harm. They could emphasize the fact that today many people are media literate and critically compare products before they buy them. On the other hand they could point out that a change in advertising campaigns is always refreshing and that they have given thought to a product they would never have considered buying otherwise.

**2.** The role play should make clear the conflict the travel agent is in and, for example, the legal consequences that may arise when he deliberately tells lies. It can train students to be inquisitive and ask questions to the point. When reflecting upon the sales interview students should not only state feelings like 'enthusiastic' or 'helpless' or 'torn between shame and necessity', they should be made aware where they themselves used slogans, superlatives, etc. during the interview and at what point the customers felt convinced/the agent felt that he had convinced the customers.

**3. Activity**

In preparation of the panel discussion and/or creating of anti-ads students can do research on the Internet or watch the film *Crazy people* from which the ads on Worksheet 25 were taken. In a debate students can assume the position of consumer protection groups, CEOs of advertising agencies, consumers and representatives of the media being dependent on adverts as a means of financing their newspapers, etc. Each group can have two minutes to state their point of view.
Topics could be: A world without adverts? Should ads be prohibited? Or 'Anti-ads – a means to alter consumer behaviour?' Each speaker can jot down his arguments on a flipchart, transparency or large sheet of paper.
Some of the following pros and cons could be mentioned:

| Pros of advertising | Cons |
|---|---|
| • provides information (not only about a product you already know but also about products that have never been on the market before)<br>• anti-ads inform about side effects of products or behaviour thus having a pedagogical effect<br>• creates jobs (in advertising agencies as well as firms that reach their target groups better) | • seduces, convinces, persuades consumers to buy sth they do not even want<br>• not being informed about a product is consumer protection in itself<br>• people buy lots of unnecessary items thus jeopardising worldwide resources and generating a lot of waste |

# Dennis Hopper – *Easy Rider* (1969) and Ford Cougar

## Born to be wild

Automobile companies cast Hollywood celebrities in TV commercials to promote their cars.

**1.** Analyse the given film stills from www.youtube.com/watch?v=Sd5DmKNxICQ and explain in what way they allude to major Hollywood successes.

**2.** Create your own commercial, using film stills from famous movies and stars (e.g. *Men in Black* to promote leather coats, *Spider Man* – glue, *Psycho* – bathroom equipment, *The Beach* – suntan lotion, *Titanic* – rescue equipment/life belts, etc.). Your commercial can be funny, romantic, ironical, thrilling or/and entertaining …
Promote a product of your own choice.

**3.** Search the Internet and find out about further TV commercials like this given one, e.g.:

- http://de.youtube.com/watch?v=Q7edm5fkD1E (Sean Connery and Citroen C6)
- http://de.youtube.com/watch?v=M4FVpWd219Q (Dustin Hoffman and Audi A6)

# Campaigns that went wrong

## False promises

SPECIAL ADVERTISING SECTION

**INDIA** Meeting the Global Marketplace

### Journey to Beyond:

India Is a Magnet for the World's Tourists...and the Facilities That Serve Them

By Debashis Basu

Blessed with the world-famous Himalayas, a long and scenic coastline, and one of the world's seven wonders—the Taj Mahal—India has long been a source of fascination, and a travel destination of choice. In fact, tourist demand for India is so great the Indian government projects the demand for a million guest rooms to service some 5 million tourists annually by 2000.

*The Taj Mahal: One of the world's seven wonders*

The country's cachet for tourists has paid dividends to those in the hotel and restaurant industries; and for workers throughout the country this booming sector has been a steady source of jobs. In fact, to cater to the steady demand, domestic players have been making future plans, thanks to the entry of global hospitality majors into the country. Consider this:

·Radisson Hotels International is entering into a joint venture with Unitech Ltd. to manage future Radisson hotels in India.

· Carlson Companies Inc., the world's largest conglomerate in the leisure and travel industry, has eight new hotel projects under construction. Carlson is also planning to launch its restaurant chain—Italianni—in India sometime soon.

·Marriott International. Inc. of the U.S. is looking into managing hotels in Mumbai, Chennai, Delhi and Calcutta in the next three years.

If investment by multinationals has boosted the Indian economy as a whole, it has also been healthy for the local competition. "I welcome the entry of major players into the Indian market," says R. K. Krishna Kumar, managing director, Taj group of hotels. "It will help us to become better and more efficient."

Indeed, in response to looming competition from foreign players, Indian hotel companies have already started streamlining operations. A new division at the Taj Group, with a chain of some 45 hotels, for instance, now monitors service quality and defines operational standards.

Committed to this vital sector, the government has gotten into the act as well. Recently, the sector has been exempted from the 10 percent duty other industries must pay to import goods, essential since hotels must continually import equipment to deliver world-class amenities. And, with the Indian Tourism Ministry estimating the need for Rs. 4 bn in investment over the next four years, a special government fund will supplement the influx of private investment dollars already rolling in. ■

Newsweek, December 14, 1998, p. 46

After the SARS virus outbreak the campaign was changed:

Hong Kong Tourist Board, December 2005

### India without the slogans

By the time we got to our hotel there was no power to run the air-conditioning. We pressed on until we reached another lodge. This time there was power, but no cell-phone signal. A series of hiccups would have been par for the course in India a decade or so ago. But then came the outsourcing and high-tech booms and marketing campaigns like "Incredible India", and suddenly India's image had gone from pauper to looming global player. Except the reality hasn't. [...] The lack of progress wouldn't be so noticeable if India's marketing gurus hadn't raised expectations so high. Last years at the world Economic Forum in Davos, Switzerland, India's government and industries backed a publicity campaign dubbed "India Everywhere", which overwhelmed conference attendees with facts and figures about the wonderful new India. But since I arrived in India [...] I have heard countless foreign businessmen and women in New Delhi and Mumbai (formerly Bombay) complaining about the gap between the image India projects and the reality. [...] I knew India was still poor and frustrating as well as fascinating and exciting and full of great stories. I have found all those things, but I have also realized that parts of Africa have better services and infrastructure than India, and just as good prospects for development. It's just that Africa hasn't yet come up with a catchy slogan to sell itself. I hope it doesn't. Better to be surprised than disappointed.

Simon Robinson, TIME Magazine, June 4, 2007, p. 64

# Overrun by success



**Sometimes merchandising-accessories become more famous than the product itself. Currently, Audi is contesting the popularity of the well-known "Shaky Elvis" puppet.**

Lately Joachim Cordshagen, 44, appears stressed out because he feels unchallenged. He studied political science and organizational psychology and is now responsible for Audi's "Communication, Business and Economy" department in Ingolstadt, Bavaria. So Cordshagen is of some importance. At least, he is definitely no joke article salesman – even though he has been responding to customers' demands for a warped plastic doll for weeks.

When would "Shaky Elvis" be up for grabs? At what price? Where could he be ordered? And rather than reporting soaring sales figures for Audi, Cordshagen instead has to admit that the ad hoc established service-hotline is continuously breaking down under the barrage of doll fans.

The group had launched a TV and cinema commercial spot in early in March [2001], promoting the new multitronic (CVT) automatic transmission. Message: this car doesn't buck, it coasts.

So then – the commercial shows a pudgy Elvis Presley look-a-like, waiting for a lift at the roadside, after his old American wreck of a car conks out. It is, of course, an attractive young woman driving an Audi who stops for him. The elderly rocker puts up his little Shaky Elvis on the front windshield because the little Shaky Elvis always jiggles along to the shifting of the gears. But there is no jiggling in an Audi – except for in the marketing department because, since then, everyone want this little jumble sale accessory with the suction cup. Audi would not be the scrupulously organized German car producer that it is, if it could not develop even this model for serial production in no time. By early June, the first delivery of a "limited edition" of 15,000 examples (at a collector's price of 8 Euros plus delivery costs) is expected on the German market. Planning for the "middle term", Cordshagen already expects to be able to increase sales tenfold.

Before even being available, the puppets were already being offered by online companies such as Ebay at black market prices of about 50 Deutschmark [about 27 €]. Even forgeries have already been circulated, Cordshagen explains.

As it had actually been designed exclusively for the film shooting in South Africa, the original is legally protected – and Audi's property. Whereas the trade name "Shaky Elvis" is not, of course. On the contrary, all involved are anxious to avoid any reference to the King of Rock'n'Roll. The Presley heirs had apparently previously demanded 1,5 million Deutschmark [0.8 Million €] for legal rights. To avoid expenses of this order, the doll got untypical-Elvis blond hair and, for the commercial's background music, Roger Miller's oldie "King of the Road".

It has all taken on "a life of its own", comments Audi manager Cordshagen, with regard to both the nickname and the neo-kitsch hype.

Although even Audi should have anticipated being bowled over (literally) by the success of the commercial. This has happened repeatedly in the history of advertising; side props have gained the upper hand, and far greater popularity than the product itself. These range from "Lurchi" who quickly outranked the footwear from Kornwestheim [Salamander shoes], and made a career as bendy rubber hero and children's books protagonist, to Aral's "nodding dog" [*Wackeldackel*]. [...]

However, whenever such an effect is deliberately intended, it is most likely to be a flop. In 1999 Levi's let "Flat Eric" loose in Germany. It cost the company about 30 million Deutschmark to position the fluffy yellow Muppet copy, "Lurchi" for the rap generation. Then came the CD. Next came production of the toy. And then the game was up. Levi's had simply sold less pairs of jeans than ever before. The jeans' brand name had taken second place. "When the gag is stronger than the product," Volker Nickel from the central association of the German advertising industry explains, "this is called the 'vampire effect'." The prop intended to support the product sucks the shine out of the brand itself. Who remembers the whisky brand "Johnny Walker" behind all the funny capers of the grouse [*Moorhuhn*]? In terms of "vampire effects" this game hit the jackpot.

Iris Edelbrock and Alexandra Rieb, translated from Thomas Tuma, „Vom Erfolg überrollt" in: Der Spiegel, 22/2001, 28.05.2001, p. 94

# Creating images in politics – Assembling and disassembling of facts

Poster for the General Election in GB, 1931

Newsweek, September 21, 1998

Newsweek, September 18, 2006

Newsweek, August 24, 1998

Newsweek, September 18, 2006

Time, May 21, 2007

# Now you are the candidate!

Imagine you are the candidate a) for the presidency.
b) as a mayor.
c) for the city council.
d) chief executive of a company.
e) ...

- Create slogans to draw attention to your political aims.
- Consider important topics the voters are concerned about such as: pollution, health care, (public) expenses, (rising) taxation, energy, problems of migration, etc.
- It is possibly necessary to play down certain touchy topics or even cover something up that might damage your public image or endanger the success of the campaign.

**Useful tips and tricks**

- employ rhetorical questions ... and answer them ...
- use key symbols (freedom, peace)
- use different grammatical persons: we, us → patterns of solidarity; they, they → patterns of distinction
- employ emotionally loaded words
- catch the listeners by surprise – say something they don't expect
- use figurative language (metaphors, personifications → the light of hope, solid as a rock ...)
- use repetitions (e. g. alliterations, anaphora, etc.)
- address your audience personally
- give them the feeling of being part of something important

**Well-tried formulations**

- Care not cash.
- Leadership for the future!
- Prosperity for Germany's families!
- Moving our country forward!
- Let's bring people together!
- Family values/matters.
- A time for change.
- Give change a chance.
- Peace and prosperity.
- Because our people deserve better.
- For the first time, our country/city ...
- Read my lips ...
- A proof is a proof.
- Don't you worry, but ...
- There is no such thing as ...

- In a presentation, reveal your political statements to the class.

Afterwards, evaluate your presentations, deciding on which statements/slogans you considered most/least convincing/appealing, etc., and give reasons for your opinion.

# Review

**1.** Which "instincts", emotions and sentiments do the ads appeal to?

**2.** What are the target groups of the ads – and how do the ads exert influence on the viewers?

# Klausur 1

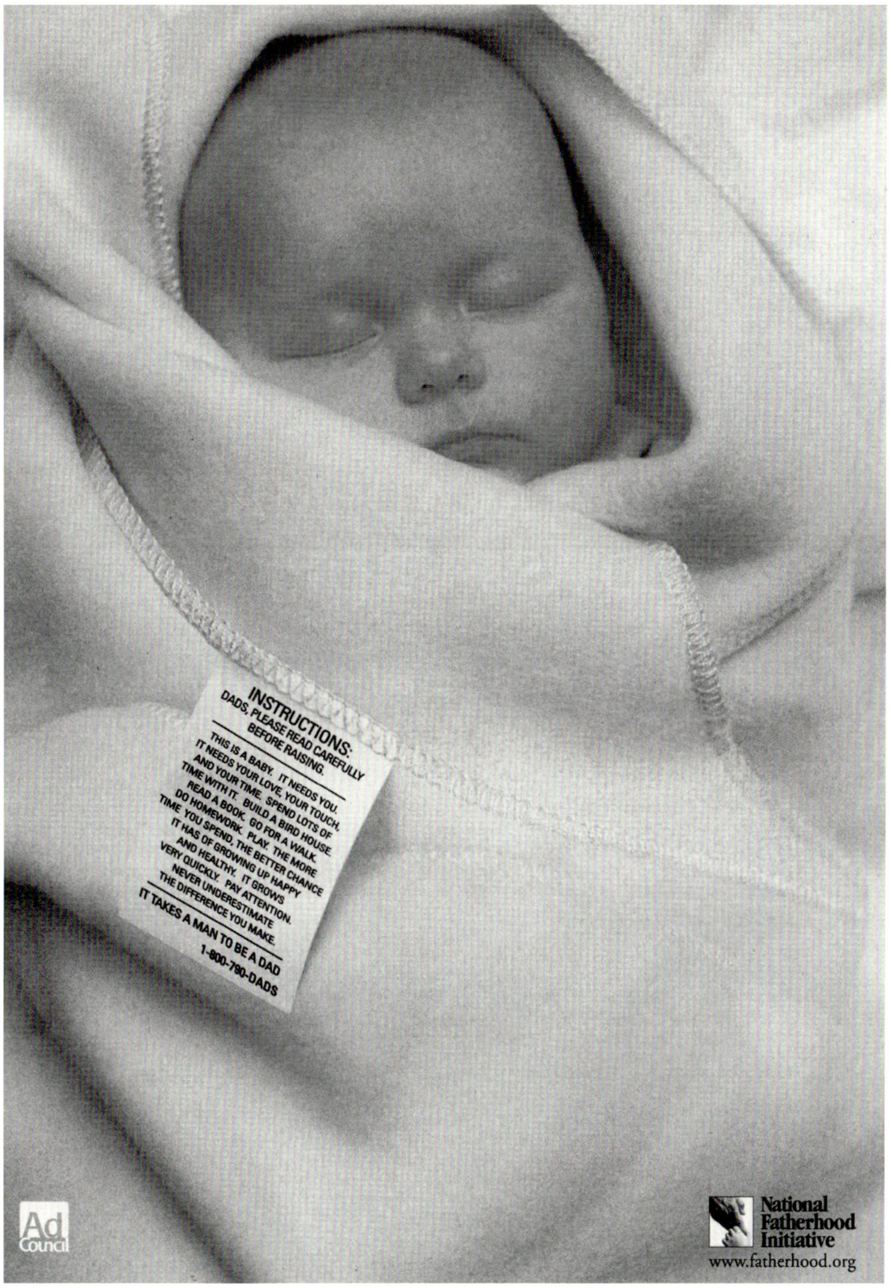


**Text from the tag:**

Instructions:
Dads, please read carefully before raising.
This is a baby, it needs you, it needs your love, your touch, and your time. Spend lots of time with it. Build a bird house. Read a book. Go for a walk. Do homework. Play. The more time you spend, the better chance it has of growing up happy and healthy. It grows very quickly. Pay attention. Never underestimate the difference you make.
It takes a man to be a dad
1-800-790-dads

**1.** Explain the basic contents and purpose of the advertisement. *(Comprehension)* — *15 credits*

**2.** Show how the desired effect is achieved by analyzing the pictorial elements and main components of the copy. *(Analysis)* — *25 credits*

**3.** Critically comment on this way of promoting the duty of parental care and the needs of children in particular, and the responsibility of the media in general. *(Comment/Evaluation)* — *20 credits*

*Total:* *60 credits*

**1. Contents and purpose of the advertisement**

The eye-catcher of the ad is a cute, little sleeping baby (→ scheme of childlike characteristics) that is snuggled up in a white (→ innocence) blanket to which a tag is attached. At first sight this tag seems to provide the washing instructions for the blanket. At a second glance, the text on the tag turns out to be the body copy of the ad, revealing "instructions"/ advice for fathers on how to raise their children. In the lower right corner is the label/logo of the "company": National Fatherhood Initiative – as well as the initiative's Internet address. The overall atmosphere conveyed by the ad is friendliness, cosiness and safety: it subconsciously appeals to people's protective instinct and the message expressed in the clear instructions given to the fathers is to take over responsibility and to take care of their child in order to improve the child's chance to lead a happy and healthy life. It encourages men/fathers especially, to take their child's education seriously.

**2. Pictorial elements and main components of the copy and their function**

- **The illustration/eye-catcher:**
  a cute, sleeping little baby snuggled up in a white blanket (→ use of soft colours)
  → aims at emotionalizing the viewer who (of course) is attracted (protective instincts)
  → The white blanket and the pink skin of the baby convey an atmosphere of cosiness/safety/peace.

- **Further components of the ad:**
  - There is an **element of surprise:** the tag (which provides the instructions, not for the blanket but for the baby); humorous allusion to the "helplessness" of men/fathers who are (often) given instructions an how to use certain gadgets in the household ("This is a baby." → **irony**)
  - use of **contrast**: human warmth/care vs. technical instruction; "it grows very quickly" vs. "spend more time"
  - The **logo** of the initiative in the (traditionally) right lower corner underlines the aspect of care/human warmth: the hand of a male adult extended to a child's hand. The Internet address next to the logo facilitates contacting the initiative easily for further information.
  - The **body copy** employs certain statements and **keywords/catchphrases**:

| | | |
|---|---|---|
| it needs ... | never underestimate | it needs you ... your |
| lots of time | pay attention | dads ... read carefully |
| better chances | build a birdhouse | the difference you make |
| love ... being happy | spend lots of time | it takes a man |
| (growing up) healthy | read a book | |
| care ... touch | do homework | |
| ⇓ | ⇓ | ⇓ |
| **human needs/baby's needs** | **parental duty/care/responsibility** | **emotion/appeal to fathers in particular** |

  - **direct appeal** to the reader by **the use of repetition** (pronouns you/your); short statements and **orders** (it has to ..., play ..., read ..., go ...); use of climax (the more ... the better ...)
  - **The target group** the ad appeals to are presumably (young) families and fathers; the ad reminds them of their parental duties and responsibility – it indirectly also appeals to their conscience.
  - In all, the picture conveys a harmonious atmosphere (friendly light/soft colours, a peacefully sleeping baby).
  - employment of the AIDA model: Attention (baby, tag), Interest (tag, the baby, logo), Desire (evoking and arousing emotion/concern), Action (appeal to care/feel responsible, appeal to get informed → company homepage)

**3. Critical comment an advertising parental care and the needs of children/the responsibility of the media**

- Discussion of the responsibility of the media – should ads use children/babies? Should the topic of parental care, etc. be promoted in the media at all?
- Possible reference to neglected children and the problem of domestic violence; can ads like this one, commercials or media publicity prevent these horrifying crimes?
- General criticism: to what extent do/should ads/commercials (ab-)use the viewer's fears and emotions?

# Klausur 2

## Are the women in Dove's new ad campaign too big to sell beauty products, or have our minds gotten too small?

Even if you haven't seen Dove's "Campaign for Real Beauty", you've probably heard about it. The ads promote a new line of skin-firming creams and feature six "regular" women of varying sizes and ethnicities cheerfully posing in plain white underwear. The curvy non-model models were introduced by Dove in June, but newspapers across the country are still simmering with duelling diatribes about Dove's selection of women who are neither skinny nor camouflaged in sexy clothes. Everyone seems to have an opinion about whether the women are a revolutionary rejection of the super-thin media ideal, or just nice girls who are too chubby to be up on billboards wearing next to nothing.

Dove marketing director Kathy O'Brien says that the company wants the ads to "change the way society views beauty", and "provoke discussion and debate". They have certainly succeeded in provoking people. There is a surprising amount of hostility in some reactions to the ads. Lucio Guerrero, a staff reporter for the Chicago Sun-Times who was apparently offended by the sight of the ads on his commute, wrote an July 19: "Really, the only time I want to see a thigh that big is in a bucket with bread crumbs on it." Guerrero may have won himself a spot as the Ann Coulter of ad commentary, but there were also critical remarks by same female writers indignant because Dove had the nerve to sell anti-cellulite potions while saying that women should feel beautiful just the way they are. With the word fat being used so liberally in national publications (where did political correctness go?), the campaign could also be in danger of creating a backlash that hurts its efforts to change the wafer-thin definition of attractive. [...]

Meanwhile, Slate.com's Seth Stevenson says that the campaign, noble or not, is bad business because eventually it will doom Dove as the "brand for fat girls". But are these women fat? Or, are we just so conditioned by Victoria's secret-style bodies that a size 8 looks big? Dove says their models are in their 20s and range from size 6 to size 12. The average American woman is somewhere between a 12 and 14 according to a 2004 survey by SizeUSA (a project sponsored by Target and JCPenny stores among others). This puts the Dove girls on the smaller side of normal. And certainly, one would assume that no one is calling them "fat" in their other lives as teachers, wives and café baristas.

The shock value of Dove's reality ads might have more to do with the way the campaign was shot than the weight of the models. While photographer Jan Rankin may have been going for a refreshing, natural look, the unretouched photos turned out to be the equivalent of full-length passport shots of women in what looks like underwear meant for jogging. One has to ask whether even celebrity beauties like Jennifer Lopez, Beyoncé Knowles or Kate Winslet would inspire the same harsh critiques under those less-than-flattering conditions.

[Ann] Kearney-Crooke [author and expert on female body image] says that the fact that the women are not posed provocatively in alluring push-up bras is precisely why the ads are so good for female the self-image. "What I love is that these women look like they're having fun. They're connected to each other and they don't look like objects – which is important since objectification can lead to violence against women." *(581 words)*

Susanna Schrobsdorff, in Newsweek online, Aug. 5, 2005, www.msnbc.msn.com/id/8813128 [22.11.2006]

**1.** Summarize the given article, paying attention to the controversial views. *(Comprehension)* *20 credits*

**2.** With reference to the author's main intention, analyse the structural and stylistic devices employed to convey the controversial attitudes as well as her own view of "beauty and size". *(Analysis)* *20 credits*

**3.** After reading this article excerpt published in *Newsweek* (online), you, as a reader, are given the opportunity of commenting on the aspects discussed. Write a "letter to the editor", stating your opinion on the discussed matter. *(Comment/(Re-)creation of text)* *20 credits*

*Total:* *60 credits*

# Klausur 2: Erwartungshorizont

**1.** The article written by Susanna Schrobsdorff, Newsweek (online) Aug. 5, 2005 deals with Dove's new campaign to promote beauty products with the help of photos of normal to slightly overweight women. Whereas the ads should boost women's self-confidence and thereby be an antidote to anorexic models, the campaign has met criticism from both male reporters as well as female writers pointing out that the ads could fire back at Dove's – rather hypocritical – firm philosophy, sales figures and newly established female confidence. The firm however defends its strategy and emphasizes that – because of not focussing on women as sex objects – the photos may reduce violence against women.

**2.** By using 'why' and 'controversial' in the headline the author makes clear from the start that the article will use analysis as well as 'juxtaposition' to show the different points of view. This is further ernphasized in the subheading (provocative rhetorical question.) Throughout the text she makes use of conjunctions ('but' l. 4, l. 18 and 'or' l. 7, l. 19 – here in combination with a rhetorical question).

Quoting 'experts' to give arguments a voice and allow a view on the different facets, the author nevertheless adds ironic remarks (l. 12 – Guerrero may have won himself a spot as the Ann Coulter of ad commentary; l. 14 female writers indignant, (l. 16) where did political correctness go?). Alliterations like 'duelling diatribes' (l. 4), 'revolutionary rejection' (l. 6), 'bad business' (l. 18), 'provoking people' (l. 9) add both to her entertaining style and the ironical/critical view on the opponents. Her choice of words, from 'fat' (l. 15, l. 20, l. 24) to 'chubby' (l. 7) or 'curvy' (l. 3) are contrasted by 'wafer-thin' (l. 17), 'skinny' (l. 5), 'super-thin', (l. 6). Throughout the article it becomes apparent that the author distinguishes clearly between 'real size' and 'beauty' and how ads make women appear to be. The 'natural' (ll. 26f.) look of 'non-model models' is as similarly artfully created as the look of women like Jennifer Lopez or Kate Winslet and other models 'posed provocatively in alluring push-up bras' (l. 32). Although it becomes clear that the author does not opt for the common practice of advertisement to use uncommonly beautiful or thin models she nevertheless doubts the sincerity of the Dove campaign to create 'real beauty' and thereby fight for new female confidence.

**3.** Students can, for example, take the point of view that the Dove campaign was long overdue. More and more women are absolutely dissatisfied with their bodies and – just to keep a slim waistline – go on dieting eternally or many young girls are critically anorexic because of severe eating disorders. Even if Dove might misuse women's wishes to accept themselves as they are – this might be better than doing nothing and exposing people to severe health problems.

Or they can comment on Guerrero's statement: 'the only time I want to see a thigh that big is in a bucket with bread crumbs in it' (l. 12) as being really chauvinistic. 'Sex sells' is not only used in adverts of all kinds of products – it has also destroyed the self-confidence of women not being able to live up to the kind of beauty ideal that has been promoted. However they can share the author's point of view that even Dove uses this – if only the other way round.

**Note: The teacher might want to explain the following names/expressions:**

l. 13 *Ann Coulter:* an American, highly disputed conservative columnist, political commentator and author
l. 18 *Slate.com:* an online news and culture magazine founded by Microsoft, since 2004 run by the Washington Post
l. 20 *Victoria's Secret:* a retailer of lingerie, women's clothing and beauty products, well known for its fashion shows which feature supermodels
l. 22 *Target, JCPenny:* chains of US department and retail stores, mostly located in suburban shopping malls
ll. 21 ff. *sizes US-German:* 6 = 32, 8 = 34, 10 = 36, 12 = 38, 14 = 40, 16 = 42, 18 = 44

**Note: Transparency 2 provides a colour print of the National Fatherhood Initiative ad.**